EDUCATING ABOUT ALCOHOL
Professional perspectives and practice in South West England

Robin Means
Lyn Harrison
Lesley Hoyes
Randall Smith

Occasional Paper 25

UNIVERSITY·OF·BRISTOL
SCHOOL·FOR·ADVANCED·URBAN·STUDIES

The School for Advanced Urban Studies was established jointly by the University of Bristol and the Department of the Environment in 1973 as a post-experience teaching and research centre in the field of urban policy. In addition to the dissemination of material in courses and seminars the School has established three publications series: **SAUS Studies, Occasional Papers and Working Papers.**

General enquiries about the School, its courses, research programme and publications may be addressed to the Publicity Secretary.

School for Advanced Urban Studies
Rodney Lodge
Grange Road
Clifton
Bristol BS8 4EA

Telephone: (0272) 741117

Director: Professor Murray Stewart

CONTENTS

ACKNOWLEDGEMENTS

An enormous number of people have supported the production of this Occasional Paper. First, we must thank the Health Education Council for funding the research that enabled us to carry out the locality studies described in the paper, and for their comments on an early draft. Second, we have to thank those involved in the development of the alcohol education programme in South West England: the programme staff, members of the Management Group, and the Regional Advisory Committee. Third, we acknowledge the vital help given us by the 173 people who gave up their time to talk with us, and those other people who gave us advice on whom we should contact. Fourth, the research secretary staff, in particular Frances Wiggins and Doreen Field, who have dealt with our manuscripts with patience beyond the call of duty. Fifth, Julie Platt, the School's Publications Officer who has guided us with tact, efficiency and discretion in the preparation of the Occasional Paper itself.

We hope that the reader will not think their efforts have been in vain. Any errors, as well as expression of opinions, are of course the joint responsibility of the authors.

Robin Means
Lyn Harrison
Lesley Hoyes
Randall Smith   March 1986

1

THE S.W. ENGLAND ALCOHOL EDUCATION PROGRAMME AND THE LOCALITY RESEARCH

Background

The South West England alcohol education programme has been in existence since April 1984 and at the time of fieldwork for this report was staffed by a Co-ordinator and Deputy Co-ordinator, both of whom were funded by the Health Education Council (HEC) but based in local agencies. For the purposes of the programme, the HEC saw the South Western Regional Health Authority as the most appropriate operational definition of the region. It was also decided to include the Bath District Health Authority, much of which is within Avon, and the West Dorset District Health Authority, which in terms of media coverage can be regarded as part of the South West. Thus, the region as defined by this educational programme covers the five counties of Cornwall, Devon, Somerset, Avon and Gloucester, plus a part of Wiltshire and a part of Dorset.

The HEC has also funded a research team at the School for Advanced Urban Studies (SAUS), University of Bristol to help in the evaluation of this programme. This team set itself two main tasks in its initial research proposal to the HEC. These were:

(a)   The collection and interpretation of data which will help to direct the South West alcohol education programme in the setting of objectives

(b)   The collection and interpretation of data which will help in the evaluation of the overall programme.

One important mechanism for achieving these tasks took the form of four locality studies. Between 30 and 55 meetings were held with professional and voluntary workers in each of these areas. An important lesson from the previous alcohol education campaign in the North East was the need to gear messages about sensible drinking to the requirements of specific localities and specific groups. The evaluation report [1] for this campaign stressed that an awareness of policy implementation issues was essential.

1

Structures to disseminate information about sensible drinking and counselling services for those with particular needs would develop and be maintained beyond the impetus of the campaign only if a wide range of 'professionals' on the ground was convinced of the need for alcohol education in their localities. In this context, the report takes a very wide definition of 'professional' to mean paid and unpaid workers who provide specific services in their localities.

It was, therefore, hoped that the locality studies would help staff involved in the South West alcohol education programme in the setting of objectives that overcame or at least minimised these problems. These four studies would also provide a detailed account of alcohol education structures at the local level prior to the public launch of the programme. So it would be possible to return to these areas in 18 months' time to assess what impact the programme had had upon activity at the fieldwork level through re-interviewing the same respondents.

Chapters 2 to 5 of this Occasional Paper outline the initial findings from the four locality studies. Chapter 6 attempts to draw out emerging themes and issues. A special emphasis is placed upon the gap between how alcohol education issues are conceptualised by the programme and how they are conceptualised by many of our respondents.

The philosophy of the South West alcohol education programme

Programme staff spent much of their time in the first 12 months talking to many of the numerous relevant agencies in this very large geographical area. This helped the Co-ordinator and Deputy Co-ordinator to produce an Action Plan and Information Pack in Spring 1985 and the intention was that this should be a focal point for a series of local briefing conferences on the aims and philosophy of the programme. Nine such local conferences took place in 1985 following the publication of the Action Plan and Information Pack.

The Action Plan is very clear about both the philosophy and aims of the South West alcohol education programme. The plan stresses the need for a social learning approach to alcohol education because this kind of approach recognises the individual's right to choose, the importance of participative forms of learning and the need to locate alcohol issues within the broader question of health and health promotion. The Action Plan claims that seven implications flow from an acceptance of such a philosophy for the programme:

1.   Education, policies and programmes should focus on everyone, not just on the minority with serious drinking problems.

2.   Individuals should be given the opportunity to identify what sensible drinking means for them.

3.   Drinking alcohol has benefits and costs and each person can be helped to identify these for themselves, in order to make their choices.

4.   The benefits of drinking can be obtained in other ways and people can be helped to identify and choose alternatives.

5.   People can be helped to understand themselves and why they drink in the way they do and this will help them to make drinking choices.

6.   Each individual or member of that family could be given information about how to help those who are drinking too much, or drinking in a way likely to harm themselves or others. Helpful tactics can be learned.

7.   Most people who find that their drinking is beginning to cause harm, or get out of control, can re-establish social drinking or learn to be abstinent, many without special help. A significant minority require long-term help and effective help is available.

The Action Plan then goes on to specify that such a programme requires a major training initiative for health promoters. The main mechanism for achieving this was to be the South Western Dissemination Programme for what is known as the Drinking choices manual. This manual[2] was developed by Ina Simnett, Linda Wright and Martin Evans for the Health Education Council and the Teacher's Advisory Council on Alcohol and Drug Education (Tacade). This manual is consistent with a social learning approach because of its emphasis that individuals are responsible for their own learning and for their own choices and actions. This manual also offers 'a participating group work approach, focusing on learning rather than teaching'.[3]   The dissemination programme involves a series of residential Key Tutor training courses, the first three of which have been completed at the time of writing. The Action Plan defines Key Tutors as 'people with existing training responsibilities in the field of health/alcohol education'. These tutors would then run their own courses for local alcohol educators who would in turn run courses for clients, 'thus building a pyramidal structure'.[4]

The philosophy and approach of the South West alcohol education programme might be seen as controversial by many of those involved in alcohol education. Above all, such a philosophy rejects the disease model of alcohol abuse in which the 'alcoholic' is seen as suffering from a disease that involves a 'loss of control' so that a single drink might trigger off a psychobiological need for more and more alcohol. This model perceives the 'alcoholic' as different from the excessive drinker and who can only be saved by complete abstinence. This remains the position of most Alcoholics Anonymous groups and it is a view that continues to be popular amongst some medical practitioners and some staff and members of councils on alcoholism. An important alternative to the disease model is that offered by the concept of an alcohol dependence syndrome which was defined by the World Health Organisation in 1977 in the following terms:

> "a state, psychic and usually also physical, resulting from taking alcohol, characterised by behavioural and other responses that always include a compulsion to take alcohol on a continuous or periodic basis in order to experience its psychic effects, sometimes to avoid the discomfort of its absence; tolerance may or may not be present."[5]

Shaw et al in Responding to drinking problems[6] explain that one justification for this change of terminology was that it rejected the view that it was possible to divide drinkers up into 'alcoholics' and 'non-alcoholics' and replaced it with a stress that alcohol abuse problems existed along a continuum. However, Shaw et al point out that both the disease theory of alcoholism and the alcohol-dependence syndrome:

> "implied that the assessment and response to a drinking problem came primarily under medical jurisdiction. Like alcoholism, the alcohol-dependence syndrome was something from which one 'suffers'; it was 'diagnosed' and required 'treatment'."[7]

The Action Plan of the South West alcohol education programme, on the other hand, asserts that alcohol is everybody's business. Everyone needs to understand the good and bad effects of alcohol and everyone has the potential to be an alcohol educator.

4

The 'costs' and 'benefits' of alcohol

The main objective of the alcohol education programme in the South West is to stimulate informed debate which it is believed will in turn lead to sensible drinking. The 'balance sheet' of costs and benefits for alcohol production, sale and consumption has been well rehearsed through a number of publications dating from the late 1970s. The South West programme can then be seen as encouraging a continuation of this debate and of the policy implications, as well as the personal choices, which flow from it.

Alcoholic beverages are based upon ethyl alcohol, which is a compound of carbon, hydrogen and oxygen. Ethyl alcohol is a depressant so that, as Shaw et al point out in <u>Responding to drink problems:</u>

> "What alcohol actually does is to sedate some of the faculties of mental activity, particularly the experience of self-perception, self-criticism and fatigue. Thus whilst the person appears to himself to be operating more efficiently, in fact his performance is being impaired. But when the task in hand is carrying out a social function or making conversation, trying to impress someone, or coping with an anxiety - provoking situation, the deadening of self-criticism may be highly beneficial. Alcohol may often relieve anxiety which might have impaired performance altogether. Since alcohol depresses our inhibitions, the shy person may become forward, the quiet person become talkative and the uncertain become confident." [8]

However, Shaw et al point out that this is complicated by a variety of factors. Behaviour when intoxicated is influenced by cultural expectations so that, for example, intoxicated men are likely to behave on the whole differently from intoxicated women. Second, the regular consumption of alcohol over long periods leads to a tolerance to the intoxicating effect of alcohol. Third, the highly tolerant drinker is likely to experience withdrawal symptoms when the body has completed the process of coping with the latest intake of alcohol. In withdrawal, the drinker may "experience gross anxieties and fears, sometimes of an hallucinatory nature." [9]

There is wide agreement amongst alcohol educators and researchers about the harm that can be caused by alcohol. Nearly all would agree that chronic heavy drinkers will damage their heart, liver and brain although there appears to be far less medical agreement about the point at which damage begins to occur. Some believe that alcohol is associated with a much wider range of health problems including stomach ulcers, inflammation of the pancreas and some cancers. For example, the 1979 report of the Royal College of Psychiatrists on <u>Alcohol and alcoholism</u> p 85 stated that "at levels below those associated with alcohol dependence, there is an increased risk of cancers of the oesophagus and pharynx."[10]

Other alcohol researchers have concentrated upon the relationship of alcohol to a wide range of safety issues and social problems. Saunders has reviewed this evidence and stated that alcohol is "variously associated with":

> 80% of deaths from fire;
> two thirds of <u>parasuicides;</u>
> 62% of serious head injuries in males;
> over 50% of homicides (with nearly 50% of the victims also being intoxicated);
> 45% of fatal road traffic accidents involving young people;
> 36% of road traffic accidents involving pedestrians;
> one third of all domestic accidents;
> 30% of non-traffic accident fatalities;
> 30% of drownings.[11]

Alcohol has also been claimed to be a significant factor in many divorces, burglaries, child abuse situations, juvenile vandalism and work absence. McDonnell and Maynard[12] have estimated that alcohol misuse many have cost England and Wales over £1,600 million in 1983.

While these medical and social statistics variously related to alcohol abuse tend to focus on the costs resulting from individuals' choices, two publications in particular have located alcohol in a wider political context. The Central Policy Review Staff[13] examined in some detail the policy implications for central government related to alcohol production and consumption. It identified two crucial relationships from the statistical data. These were that alcohol related problems rise with overall increases in national consumption of alcohol and that the relative cost of alcoholic drinks had fallen during this century. It therefore recommended that the government should ensure that the price of alcohol does not fall in real terms by increasing the level of taxation so that the retail price remains at least in line with the overall retail price index.[14]

Drinking sensibly,[15] one of the series of DHSS pamphlets on prevention and health, also considers the complex relationships between alcohol production and consumption and various government departments. It stresses the need to strike a balance between, on the one hand, preventing individuals from damaging themselves or others, through the use of fiscal and social sanctions aimed at restricting the use of alcohol and on the other hand, undue restriction of individual freedom and the benefits derived from the consumption of alcohol in terms of employment, investment, exports and revenues to the government. These are issues which are not easily resolved and "the precise role the Government should play in helping prevent alcohol misuse is clearly open to debate and likely to continue to be debated for a long time to come."[16]

The four localities

As already indicated, the importance of recognising and responding to local patterns of drinking was emphasised by Budd et al in the Tyne Tees Evaluation Report. With regard to the Why spoil a good thing? television advertisement by the botanist David Bellamy, they remarked:

> "....it cannot be emphasised too strongly that the 1981 phase of the Tyne Tees campaign cannot simply be 'transferred' elsewhere, or grafted on to an existing alcohol education framework in another region of the country. There should be little difficulty in principle in mounting an information-giving campaign of the type epitomised by David Bellamy, but far more research would need to be carried out on the information and messages appropriate to other areas of the country and on the acceptibility of a presenter such as Bellamy in those areas...."[17]

The above statement could be interpreted to mean that it was essential for a research and evaluation team to uncover and define a South West regional style of drinking that would somehow be equivalent to the male beer drinkers addressed by David Bellamy in the North East. To some extent this might occur through the HEC funded questionnaire on 'Beliefs about alcohol' which has been carried out by SCPR; respondents were weighted to those living in the South West.[18]

7

However, it was also recognised early on that the South West as defined for the purposes of the programme was a large diverse area that was likely to contain (a) many different styles and patterns of drinking and (b) many different styles and patterns of alcohol education. The 'region' contains numerous market towns, seaside resorts, isolated rural villages and several large towns. Existing regional data on drinking patterns such as Paul Wilson's 1980 study of drinking in England and Wales,[19] the 1983 Family Expenditure Survey[20] and the 1984 General Household Survey[21] tend to present the South West as an 'average' region in terms of levels of consumption. The more interesting question seemed to be likely variations within the region both in drinking patterns and in the response and attitudes of potential alcohol educators to their local situation.

It was, therefore, decided to focus much of the initial research effort on four localities that reflected something of this diversity. The four areas chosen were:

(a) a market town which was the administrative centre for its county

(b) a group of isolated villages

(c) a market town and a nearby tourist/fishing village

(d) a large interwar council housing estate.

173 respondents were contacted in the four studies. Each respondent was asked questions on the following six themes:-

(a) What is their role and that of their organisation?

(b) Is alcohol education a significant feature of this work? Why has it been given the emphasis it has?

(c) How does the presence or absence of alcohol education relate to perceptions of drinking patterns and problems? What other values or perceptions underlie activity in this field?

(d) How do perceived drinking patterns and problems relate to other social problems and issues in the area?

(e) Are the respondents aware of or sympathetic to the South West alcohol education programme?

(f) Do they possess data on local drinking patterns?

In addition a separate piece of research was carried out by Adrian

Franklin on Pub drinking and the licensed trade[22] in two of these communities. This work involved a mapping of outlets, participant observation of drinking behaviour and the interviewing of a limited number of pub tenants, managers and owners.

Locality research always faces difficulties as to the extent to which it is necessary and possible to make both individuals and localities anonymous. Some individuals have 'unique' jobs that are difficult to obscure. A locality may have many schools, many primary health care teams and many youth clubs but there is likely to be only one Director of a Council on Alcoholism and one Adviser for Social Education in the local education authority. Second, those who are keen to work out each locality or those knowledgeable about the region may not be misled or confused by the simple use of fictitious names. Nevertheless, this report does use fictitious names for the localities and it refers to no individual by name. The research team believes that the recognition of individuals and/or localities is likely to direct the reader to focus to an unacceptable extent on the particular nature of each case study. The importance of the material in this book is that it presents the comments of a wide range of professionals working in these kinds of communities, on their perceptions of alcohol education issues and how these issues relate to their day to day work in that community.

The market town in the first locality study is, therefore, referred to as Cornford while the main village in the group of isolated villages is Breaton. The market town in the third study is called Westcross and the nearby fishing village is called Lyncombe. St Aldhelms is the name given to the large interwar council housing estate.

Finally, some comments will be made about the methodology employed in the research. Those interviewed can be split into the categories outlined in Table 1. A considerable effort was made to achieve consistency of coverage between the case studies. Under 'alcohol and specialist provision in the voluntary sector', interviews were carried out with the relevant councils on alcoholism and Alcoholics Anonymous groups in all four localities. More diversity existed with the NHS interviews because of the varying patterns of NHS involvement in alcohol education issues between the localities. Health education officers, primary health care workers, staff at treatment units, and various other consultants were all interviewed where appropriate. Under counselling services, each study included some contact with social workers and/or probation officers, church officials, marriage guidance counsellors and representatives of the Samaritans. Under the 'alcohol and the education department' section, at least one teacher from all the relevant secondary schools was interviewed together with appropriate youth workers. Local police and magistrates were interviewed in all four studies in the section 'alcohol and the law'. Trainers for the Youth Training Scheme were by far the largest group under the 'miscellaneous' section.

The first block of fieldwork was carried out for the Cornford study and certain changes were made as a result of this experience. The initial fieldwork emphasis in this study was upon uncovering the existing alcohol education networks rather than the attitudes of the less committed. A 'snowball'[23] approach was used in which the key actors suggested people from other agencies with an interest in alcohol education. This had at least two important implications. First, a high proportion of respondents were from senior management or senior practitioners rather than field level staff. The Executive Committee of the local Council on Alcoholism was a key source for locating respondents and membership of this committee tended to be chosen on the basis of organisational 'clout'. Second, the discussions concentrated on the minority of local professionals with an interest in alcohol counselling and education rather than the majority who did not. The youth leader, the church leader and the staff of a primary health care team were chosen on the basis that they were the main individuals in their field who were seen as having an interest in alcohol education issues.

The research team decided that it was equally important to make contact with professionals who had as yet expressed little interest in alcohol education issues. Do they believe alcohol education to be irrelevant to their work? Were they intimidated by the topic? The South West alcohol education programme had prioritised work with young people in the Action Plan and so a full coverage of Cornford secondary schools was carried out. Early interviews with these staff demonstrated that important and interesting material could be generated by discussions with those who were completely outside the existing network associated with the executive committee of the Council on Alcoholism.

This lesson was applied to the other three studies. The main disadvantage of this is that it can appear fairly arbitrary to choose one worker rather than another. In the St. Aldhelms and Breaton studies, the catchment area was reduced so as to limit the number

Table 1:   Respondents in the four locality studies

Subject area of respondent	Cornford	Breaton	Westcross and Lyncombe	St. Aldhelms	All four studies
Alcohol and specialist provision in the voluntary sector	5	2	6	3	16
Alcohol and the NHS	13	8	9	17	47
Counselling services and alcohol education	10	10	10	5	35
Alcohol and the education department	9	7	15	17	48
Alcohol and the law	6	3	3	3	15
Miscellaneous	0	1	4	7	12
TOTALS	43	31	47	52	173

of potentially relevant respondents. However, this tactic does not fully resolve the dilemma. One is still talking only to one teacher from a school or one GP from a primary health care team. The respondents are not, therefore, a statistical sample although the research team believe them to be fairly representative of professional views within the communities. So there is certainly no guarantee that similar professionals in other parts of the country conceptualise these issues in the same way, although many responses did seem linked to professional training and organisational role.

The following four chapters therefore provide an interesting insight into how a variety of 'professionals' perceive the potential role and value of alcohol education in their day to day work, offering a starting point for a debate about whether such perceptions vary because of differences in local drinking patterns, local professional networks, organisational role or professional training. In considering this information it is crucial to remember that these respondents will often minimise their potential role or powers in relation to alcohol education. Some of the possible reasons for this will be discussed at various points in the report but especially in Chapter 6. The potential role of all these 'professionals' in alcohol education will soon be outlined in detail through the publication of the DHSS funded research by Philip Tether and David Robinson in Preventing alcohol problems: a guide to local action.[24] This will look at many of the same groups as this report but from the point of view of their actual responsibilities and potential role. Their report will provide numerous examples of good practice. For example, Tether[25] in a paper produced for an Alcohol Concern Conference has already outlined the extent to which existing licensing laws are open to a variety of interpretations. The extent to which this may be true is not apparent from our interviews with magistrates in the four localities.

The research team has attempted to check the validity of their four locality studies through the use of respondent validation techniques,[26] defined by McKeganey and Hunter in the following terms:

"Broadly speaking respondent validation involves the attempt to explore the extent to which the subjects of a sociological description recognise themselves in, and agree to, the description as containing an accurate representation of their work."[27]

All the respondents in this study were sent either a copy of their locality report or a letter indicating such a report was available. As a result, over 100 respondents have seen their report and been given the opportunity to comment. Those who have not seen their locality report are those who provided the least used material.

As one would expect, the response was mixed although several respondents stressed how their report had "got things just about right". Others expressed more reservations although these usually revolved around the sensitivity[28] of what they said rather than the accuracy of reportage. The resultant re-drafting has probably had the effect of minimising the amount of conflict and disagreement between agencies about alcohol related problems and how they can best be tackled.

The South West alcohol education programme: the first 18 months

This report is not about the politics, process or impact of the South West alcohol education programme. Instead it focuses on the perceptions of a wide range of professionals about alcohol education. However, an important minority of our respondents were aware of the programme and some had very strong views about how it should proceed. It is, therefore, appropriate to make a few comments about some of the difficulties of the programme in the first eighteen months.

The Co-ordinator and Deputy Co-ordinator have had to try to develop a regional programme over a very large geographical area and with very limited financial resources. Support has been potentially available from a variety of sources, namely the HEC in London, the research team, their immediate employers (two different Councils on Alcoholism), a Regional Advisory Committee of over 30 members and a Planning and Monitoring Group of seven members. There was uncertainty about the respective roles of these various groups. Impossible demands were placed on the programme staff. The Co-ordinator resigned in April 1985 and the Deputy Co-ordinator in September 1985.

There is wide agreement that the original arrangements were unsatisfactory. The new Co-ordinator is expected to be placed in the Regional Health Authority. The Planning and Monitoring Group has agreed to take on a stronger management role. The programme is to be developed mainly at district health authority (DHA) level through the appointment of a rolling programme of local co-ordinators. These posts will be 50% funded by the HEC for two to three years and 50% funded by DHAs. The first two such appointments are going to be health education officers but other possibilities (eg an education officer post in a voluntary agency) have not been excluded.

References

1.   Budd, J., Gray, P. and McCron, R. (1982), The Tyne Tees alcohol education campaign: an evaluation, Health Education Council, London.

2.   Simnett, I., Wright, L. and Evans, M. (1982), Drinking choices: a training manual for alcohol educators, Tacade/HEC.

3.   Ibid, p 6.

4.   Problems in developing a 'pyramid' of alcohol educators in Tyne Tees are discussed by Brandes, D. (1985), An illuminative evaluation of an alcohol education project, Unpublished PhD, University of Durham.

5.   World Health Organisation (1977), International classification of diseases (9th Revision), WHO, Geneva.

6.   Shaw, S., Cartwright, A., Spratley, T. and Harwin, J. (1978), Responding to drinking problems, Croom Helm, London.

7.   Ibid, p 73.

8.   Ibid, p 29.

9.   Ibid, p 32.

10.   Royal College of Psychiatrists (1979), Alcohol and alcoholism, Tavistock, London, p 85.

11.   Saunders, W., 'Alcohol use in Britain: how much is too much?', Health Education Journal (1984), Volume 43, Numbers 2 and 3, pp 66-70.

12.   McDonnell, R. and Maynard, A. (1984), The costs of alcohol misuse, British Journal of Alcohol Addiction.

13. Central Policy Review Staff (1979), Alcohol policies, unpublished, May.

14. Ibid, p viii.

15. Department of Health and Social Security (1981), Prevention and health: drinking sensibly, HMSO.

16. Ibid, p 64.

17. Budd, J. et al (op cit), p 166.

18. Social and Community Planning Research, Beliefs about alcohol, Health Education Council, unpublished.

19. Wilson, P. (1980), Drinking in England and Wales, Office of Population Censuses and Surveys, HMSO, London.

20. DOE (1983), Family Expenditure Survey, HMSO, London.

21. OPCS (1984), General Household Survey 1982, HMSO, London.

22. Franklin, A. (1985), Pub drinking and the licensed trade: a study of drinking cultures and local community in two areas of South West England, School for Advanced Urban Studies, University of Bristol, Occasional Paper Number 21.

23. Hjern, B. and Porter, D. (1980), Implementation structures: a new unit of administrative analysis, International Institute of Management, mimeo, Berlin. These ideas are also discussed in Barrett, S. and Fudge, C. eds (1981), Policy and action, Methuen, London.

24. Tether, P. and Robinson, D. (1986, forthcoming), Preventing alcohol problems: a guide to local action, Tavistock, London.

25. Tether, P. (1985), Liquor licensing: its role in a local prevention strategy, paper given to Alcohol Concern's First Forum, Sheffield, 8-11 January.

26. Bloor, M. (1978), 'On the analysis of observational data: a discussion of the worth and uses of inductive techniques and respondent validation', Sociology, Volume 12, Number 3.

15

27. McKeganey, N. and Hunter, D. (1986, forthcoming), "'Only connect...'": tightrope walking and joint working in the case of the elderly', <u>Policy and Politics</u>.

28. The issue of sensitivity is discussed in Means, R. (1985), 'Some ethical and practical problems in the construction of policy recommendations from implementation research', <u>Policy and Politics</u>, Volume 10, Number 2, pp 205-215.

2
ALCOHOL EDUCATION IN CORNFORD

The locality

The following description of the Cornford locality draws heavily on
Pub drinking and the licensed trade[1] by Adrian Franklin. Cornford
is one of the two communities investigated in this study. It is an
important market town serving a wide ranging agricultural area
and also the administrative centre for the county and district
health authority. It lies on a strategic crossroads linking an
important coastal sub-region to motorway access to the North, and
linking East to West along an important coastal trunk route.
Cornford is an ancient settlement which has physical
manifestations of each major built environment surviving in
recognisable order from pre-Roman times onwards. Cornford is a
tourist centre while its beauty and proximity to both the sea and
countryside accounts for its popularity with the wealthy retired.

The local labour market in Cornford has survived the recent
recession rather well. The present unemployment rate is
substantially below the national level.

As an agricultural centre Cornford experienced overall decline in a
period prior to the recent recession and its agricultural functions
are now minimal and stabilised. Cornford is now more orientated
to providing general services for rural residents from surrounding
villages rather than playing a central role in agricultural
commerce. The county administration, hospital complexes, prison
and other state institutions are major employers, but there are also
large numbers employed in the private sector. There is a large and
expanding regional brewery and a new aero engineering factory, as
well as a shopping centre in which most national chain stores trade.
Two large cranes dominate Cornford's skyline; one is building a new
superstore, the other a large hospital building. New dwellings are
being built on the town fringe and in nearby villages.

Franklin stressed how the built environment of Cornford reflects its history and its current economic activity. Along the East-West high street axis stretches the modest tourist centre which includes many impressively restored ancient buildings. To the South lies the more modern shopping complex, to the North the concentrated sites of administrative buildings forming the Northern edge of the town. Radiating outwards and Southwards are discrete housing developments; large 19th century suburbs arranged in various sizes of house, a scattering of 1920s and 1930s privately built dwellings, two post war council estates, both of which are now extensively owner occupied and in good condition, and around the edge are large numbers of recently built, up-market private dwellings. A substantial number of professional, managerial workers and owners of businesses in Cornford commute from nearby villages.

The Cornford licensed trade and the drinking patterns of Cornford people extend beyond the municipal boundaries of the town and into these adjacent parishes. The membership of the Cornford Licensed Victuallers' Association, for instance, includes many publicans from nearby villages. All drinking outlets with a Cornford telephone exchange number were mapped. This proved to be almost equivalent to taking a three mile radius circle around Cornford's boundary and produced 71 outlets which are categorised in Table 2.

Table 2:   Licensed outlets in Cornford

Type of outlet	Number
Pubs	24
Hotels and guest houses	5
Restaurants	11
Chain and independent off licences	4
Small grocery stores	7
Supermarkets	3
Clubs	17
TOTAL	71

Franklin[2] in his study found that the majority of Cornford's licensed outlets are concentrated in the older central high street and shopping areas and in the small Victorian suburbs. This historic pattern, together with the fact that it takes only about 20 minutes to walk from one end of the town to the other - in any direction - means that there has been little incentive to build more than a handful of pubs since the town expanded in the late 19th century, although alcohol can be bought locally in these areas from grocery shops. Cornford is an old tourist centre which means the number of pubs exceeds those sustainable through purely local demand. This, too, explains why so few were built in the post 1920s suburban growth.

In Cornford, 43 people were interviewed and several meetings were also observed. Table 3 breaks these down into the appropriate categories.

Alcohol and specialist provision in the voluntary sector

(a)   The Council on Alcoholism

Meetings were held with the honorary director, chairman and senior counselling co-ordinator of the Council on Alcoholism. This organisation has had to struggle in order to establish itself financially, largely because of the caution expressed by agencies such as the health authority, social services department and probation about the most appropriate way to develop work in this area. A Council on Alcoholism for the county had been established in 1979 but was unable to secure sufficient financial support to pay full time officers. In September 1982, the Council decided to focus on the Western half of the county. The reason for this was that the district health authority in the East of the county wanted to concentrate resources in this field into its own 20 place alcohol unit. The Council on Alcoholism had a much greater prospect of obtaining financial support from the other district health authority in the form of a joint finance arrangement with the social services department. A three year grant (subject to annual review) of £12,000 per annum was obtained from April 1984. At the time of fieldwork, negotiations were taking place for a grant from the Department of Health and Social Security via Alcohol Concern which would enable the Council on Alcoholism to appoint a paid director.

Table 3: Respondents in the Cornford locality study

Subject area of respondent		Number of respondents
1. Alcohol and specialist provision in the voluntary sector	a) The Council on Alcoholism	3
	b) Self help groups	2
2. Alcohol and the NHS	a) Psychiatric services	2
	b) Senior NHS staff and health authority members	3
	c) Health education	2
	d) School of nursing	1
	e) Primary health care	5
3. Counselling services and alcohol education	a) Statutory agencies	7
	b) Voluntary agencies	2
	c) The churches	1
4. Alcohol and the education service	a) Schools	7
	b) The youth service	2
5. Alcohol and the law	a) The police	3
	b) Magistrates	3
TOTAL		43

The Council receives about 100 referrals a year for counselling help, despite their decision not to advertise this service extensively because of the shortage of counsellors. The majority of referrals were from GPs although there were also a considerable number from the Samaritans and from the probation service. Self referrals were relatively rare. The bulk of referrals were middle aged (50 plus) and/or elderly housewives. The senior counselling co-ordinator felt he offered a more relaxed service than many AA groups which tended to intimidate problem drinkers. He attempted to create a situation in which the client could release feelings; he or she was often lonely and frightened. Relaxation tapes, drinking diaries, controlled drinking and abstinence were all used as and when appropriate. However, clients were allowed to make their own decisions and the emphasis was on the offer of a caring friendship. His main task for the future was to create a network of volunteer counsellors so that a more extensive and regular service could be offered. The South West alcohol education programme would sensitise local people and so increase the demand for counselling services. Indeed, he was worried that they might be faced with an avalanche of referrals.

The Council had always been willing to provide speakers to give one-off talks on alcohol and alcohol related problems. A variety of groups had asked for speakers including the Young Farmers, Gingerbread and various women's groups. However, the Council recognised that alcohol education was very patchy and unco-ordinated. The South West alcohol education programme had underlined to them the need for a far greater emphasis upon prevention. A position paper was produced in September 1984 and this outlined the overall aim as being:

> ".....to enable members of the public to be made aware of the dangers inherent in consuming alcohol, in the hope that increased individual and community awareness may act as a preventive measure in educating and persuading people to drink sensibly in the long term. This would mean informing members of the public in a major exercise launched by the Council."

Five specific proposals were made in this paper. First, a network of counsellors should be established. Second, staff from statutory agencies should be encouraged to go on Key Tutor courses, and then they would be encouraged to form a multi-disciplinary team to help train and update professional workers in the area; the team should organise a number of one day courses for professionals in May and June 1985. Third, the public launch of the South West alcohol education programme should be followed up by the Council through the selection of 'one pilot area....' to give blanket coverage of every household and company, issuing relevant information regarding (a) That's the limit, a guide to sensible drinking, (b) a leaflet describing the Council, its functions and a list of services available, and (c) a letter from either the director or the chairman explaining the reason for the campaign. Fourth, Drinkwatch groups should be established in the pilot area so that people could learn controlled drinking through a group experience. Finally, it was suggested that the above activities needed to be monitored and evaluated.

honorary director, the chairman and the senior counselling co-
ator were all asked about their perceptions of drinking
ems and patterns in their area. The honorary director defined
olism as occurring when someone lost more than money
through drink. Alcoholism took place when one's job or homelife
was also lost, although he accepted that many experts believed it
was impossible to provide an exact definition. There were two
schools of thought about how to help such addictive drinkers,
namely abstinence or controlled drinking. Their senior counsellor
preferred the latter approach and this led to conflict with AA. The
Council on Alcoholism wished to shift its focus from the addict to
those who were only starting to become worried by their drinking.
The move from heavy social drinking to addiction might take five,
10, 15 or 20 years. The problem was grounded in the individual but
some groups were more 'at risk' than others. 'At risk' groups
included the inhabitants of isolated areas and bored housewives.
He suspected that many retired people had a drink problem,
especially if they were well off financially. However, it was hard
to be specific about the exact nature of local drinking patterns and
problems.

The senior counsellor claimed that drinking problems were spread
throughout the county and could be particularly severe in isolated
villages. Loneliness was the number one factor and this was
followed by a variety of stress related factors such as a difficult
job or the fear of losing a job. Retirement was a very important
factor, especially for those from the armed forces who were used
to an active life and found adjustment to their new situation very
difficult. He said drink was a problem for any person who
experienced social, psychological or physical problems as a result
of repeated drinking of alcohol or the drinking of others. He was
very doubtful about the value of education. He had never met
anyone who did not know that heavy drinking caused problems.
Children were intrigued to try alcohol if they received school talks
on the subject. However, he did feel that there was a need to
develop strong 'don't drink and drive' campaigns.

The chairman stressed how hard it was to reform a 'committed
alcoholic'. This group needed services but it was more important
to concentrate upon prevention and to help people avoid
alcoholism. Drink was being pushed in front of people all the time;
the tax on drink needed to be increased and availability reduced.
There was a broad spectrum of alcohol misuse in Cornford and the
Council needed to focus on all aspects, with the broad message of
'drink reasonably'. However, resources were limited and it was,

therefore, essential to harness all available support including industry, the health authority, the local authority and AA. The personnel departments of local firms needed to offer concrete help and support for people with drink problems. His own company had banned lunchtime drinking. He believed the ban had raised productivity in the afternoon, so that investment in alcohol education could be measured.

(b)   Self help groups

Meetings were held with members of both Al Anon and Alcoholics Anonymous (AA). The former explained that this self help group tried to help the worried but inexperienced partners or relatives of those with drinking problems. Such people often felt guilty because of their failure to persuade the alcoholic to seek help. People were encouraged to stay with Al Anon groups for at least six weeks and to learn fully about 'the twelve point plan'[3] based on that used by AA groups. This person said that there had been some difficulty in establishing local groups although there was now a group which met regularly in Cornford. A key stumbling block had been the lack of support from the health authority and local authority. The Al Anon group had invited all the local agencies to an open meeting in 1980 but only a single professional turned up. Most referrals come from AA or the Samaritans while one hospital social worker was particularly good at referring the partners of alcoholics. Some members joined as a result of seeing leaflets in libraries or the surgeries of local GPs. Members were mostly women and over half of the group had to travel in from outside Cornford. In recent years more parents have been coming to the group.

She felt people were 'at risk' from drink throughout Cornford society. She felt it was an 'average' drinking area in which strong family ties acted as a 'brake' for many of those tempted to abuse drink. However, teenagers were particularly 'at risk' because of the lack of social life other than public houses. Middle aged women were tempted to abuse alcohol out of loneliness when their children left home. She thought alcohol did function as a release mechanism for many people but that it became dangerous when it was needed to cope with situations, 'deaden the pain' or to help with sleep. Poor social skills were a crucial cause. There seemed to be a chemical basis to alcoholism which worked like an allergy - the first drink sets up a 'craving'. Heavy drinkers possibly progress to this state because of the toxic effects of alcohol.

She was enthusiastic about the need for more alcohol education. The general population needed to develop an increased understanding of drink related problems. Social attitudes had to be changed so that more people felt confident in not drinking at all. The television and radio had to be used to present such messages directly into the home. Professionals often failed to reach those most 'at risk' although alcohol education in schools was essential. One aim of alcohol education should be to persuade families and close friends of problem drinkers to seek earlier help. Those coming to Al Anon usually had a long history of many years of living with the problem and were very traumatised.

Her own view was that the ratios of alcohol and drug abusers in the next generation would be highest from families where the problem had existed with the parents or a parent. Al Anon helps adults affected, but children have their own insecurities and fears - by meeting in a caring/sharing group some of these can be reduced and new ways of coping emerge. Whether these groups are set up as Al Ateen or any other caring 'agency', they must be to the fore in preventative and educational work in the future.

The AA member said the Cornford group started fifteen years ago and 'peaked' at 30 per meeting around 1979. They were now down to a regular 12 to 13 attenders who came to the Thursday and Friday evening sessions. He felt such numbers were typical of rural groups and that large city groups could often attract 50 to 60 people. Only two members of his group lived in Cornford and many travelled considerable distances.[4] Membership was now 50% male and 50% female. The average age was now getting lower (around 35 years) and several people were only in their mid-twenties. This reflected better publicity about how to define drink problems and then how to respond to them. Referrals came from two main sources, namely telephone self referrals and GP advice. He claimed that some doctors were very enlightened about alcoholism but others were ignorant and did not want to know.

He claimed that AA had a far higher success rate than any other form of treatment. It was open to anyone who could admit they had a drink problem and wished to tackle it. The core of AA was 'the meeting'. AA objectives were listed, someone would speak about their drinking problems and there would be an open discussion. He said AA meetings were a unique experience and unlike any other meetings that he had attended. It was the only agency that could help with long term drinking problems. The Council on Alcoholism might be able to help those with a 'passing problem' but that was all. It was really only a talking shop.

He believed local agencies were failing to collect evidence about the level of alcohol abuse. These agencies were then able to deny there was a problem. Cornford people would claim there was a problem in other local towns but not in Cornford. However, he felt local people were involved in as much 'alcoholic drinking' as people in London. People appeared abstemious but a great deal of drink was bought through off licences and supermarkets. There was a lot of 'lace curtain' or secret drinking going on.

At the moment, alcohol was the 'hidden disease' and it was the third biggest killer of people over 18. Alcohol education was needed to make people aware of the dangers of alcohol abuse and AA were always willing to provide speakers. Social clubs needed to offer their members warnings about drink, while parents needed help in picking up the danger signs in their children. Schools should warn young people about the dangers of this mood-altering drug. He concluded with an attack on central government for its failure to tackle alcohol abuse and he blamed this on their dependence on tax revenue from drink.

Alcohol and the NHS

(a)   Psychiatric services

There are four consultant psychiatrists, each of whom takes responsibility for a specific geographical area that contains one quarter of all GPs in the district health authority. They do not specialise in particular illnesses because of the scatter of the area covered by the health authority. A meeting was held with the consultant with an interest in organising services for alcoholism. He explained that all four consultants had to be able to offer 'the psychiatry of alcoholism' and this included such diverse work as detoxification and dealing with depression. About 60 patients were sent to be 'dried out' at the only available clinic every year.

The general philosophy of this consultant was that patients with alcohol related problems should be treated in their own homes and he attempted to minimise hospital admission. However, he was really providing only first aid through an emergency drying out service and some outpatient care. For the last decade, this consultant had been attempting to develop a far more coherent service. He had encouraged the establishment of the Council on Alcoholism and he had tried to improve health authority services

25

through arguing for the creation of a Department of Alcoholism. He had taken the lead in this debate because of the existence of a gap in services rather than any particular interest in alcoholism.

He had been involved in the production of several reports that attempted to indicate the level of alcohol related health problems in the district health authority and to argue the need for improved services. In 1976, he produced a paper entitled A service for alcoholism - some proposals, in which he argued:

> "The different surveys of alcoholism throughout the British Isles indicate that about 400,000 people in England and Wales have a serious drink problem (about 11 in every 1,000 of the adult population). For this district health authority this suggests about 1,300 people in a population of 171,000."

In 1977, the planning department of the health authority carried out a postal questionnaire to all local GPs which attempted to clarify the local situation. However, only 44 GPs or 54% of those contacted bothered to reply. The subsequent report, nevertheless, felt able to claim:

> "On the basis that the general practitioners' estimate of the hidden factor is correct, and that the known sample reflects the overall pattern, 1,200 people in this district health authority have a substantial alcoholic problem, which is known (33%) or suspected (67%) by general practitioners."

Figures from both these reports were subsequently disputed by the Council on Alcoholism which claimed they underestimated the problem. The Council claimed that national data suggested that:

> "The whole county probably had in 1981 2,202 people with a severe drinking problem and 8,808 seriously affected."

The most recent report was called Time gentlemen please and was produced in February 1985 by the unit management team (mental illness services) working party on proposed services for those with alcohol problems. The working party of seven included the consultant psychiatrist and two others who had been on Key Tutor courses. The report argued that:

"National estimates suggest that alcohol is a major contributory factor in 25-30% of male admissions to psychiatric and general hospitals, and that the annual cost to the district in terms of NHS, industry, policing and traffic accidents is probably well over £10 million."

The working party argued that a clinical service needed to be established in the district health authority that was community orientated with the following two basic functions:

(i)   A specialist assessment and treatment function. This service would be aimed at any person who experienced social, psychological or physical problems as a consequence of their own drinking or the drinking of others, and would deal with referrals where possible in community settings either directly by members of a specialist team, or by non-specialist helping agencies supported by such a team.

(ii)   An educational training and support function, in partnership with other agencies. This would enable 'non-specialist personnel' to achieve better recognition and greater confidence in effecting appropriate interventions themselves.

The proposed team would work in a Department of Alcoholism and be multi-disciplinary along the lines of the community alcohol team model being developed in such areas as Exeter. The concluding note of the report stated that:

"In Autumn 1985, the Health Education Council will launch a major media campaign (in the region) aimed at raising public awareness about alcohol and alcohol problems. Judging by the impact of a similar venture in the North East of England recently, we should expect a marked increase in the numbers requesting help and being referred for help from this time. It would be unfortunate if the Health Service, through lack of resources and organisation in this matter, were unable to fulfil its obligation to make a meaningful contribution to treatment, advice and support."

At the time of writing, the research team understand that no firm decision had been made about the establishment of the Department of Alcoholism. One difficulty might be finance, although the consultant psychiatrist expressed the hope that it could be financed through resources released by the gradual transition of mentally ill people from institutions to the community.

The consultant psychiatrist was also asked for his more general perceptions of drinking patterns and problems in the Cornford area. He felt most problem drinkers were troubled people who were 'loaded with psychopathology' rather than individuals led astray by peer group acceptance of heavy drinking. However, there were not many 'serious drinkers' in Cornford and he believed the health authority knew who they were. Some professionals allowed work stress to lead them gradually into addictive drinking and physical damage. The wealthy did sometimes experience these difficulties but they soon removed themselves into the private sector. He did not feel low income was an important source of alcoholism although he had noticed that those made redundant often spent long periods in public houses. 'Down and out' drinkers usually had psychiatric disorders. He was more concerned by bored wives who drank at home in the afternoon. In general, the county had a 'dry' rather than a 'wet' culture. The health authority did not place a high priority on preventive work in the area of mental illness and he tended to assume that responsibility for health education of all kinds, including alcohol education, lay with the community physician and health education officers.

The nursing officer for the psychiatric nursing service was responsible for a team of nurses who had a total caseload of around 270. There was a turnover of about ten cases per month. An alcohol related referral occurred about once in every two months and this represented about 5% of the total. About two thirds of his team were very reluctant to become involved with alcoholics although a recently appointed staff nurse did have a strong interest. She wished to transfer to psychiatric nursing in the community and this would enable him to develop a service for those with drinking problems.

At the moment, few referrals were received because doctors realised there were no resources. At times, supervision sessions with a nurse led him to 'spot' a drink problem in a client. Much of the work with the limited number of alcohol referrals involved helping the patient cope with stress. Where appropriate such patients were referred to other agencies for help. For example, a health visitor might be asked to support a mother who was drinking. However, his central problem was that all his alcohol related work was extra to the formal requirements of his job.

He believed there were several groups 'at risk' in the Cornford area. Many people commuted into Cornford for work and left housebound wives with young children behind. Retired couples were tempted to buy a couple of bottles of sherry a week from the supermarket. Work stress was common in those working for the local authority and the health authority. Some people used drink as a mechanism for coping with a job they were not equipped to do. The above problems tended to be hidden and unseen. Cornford and the surrounding villages were not involved in the kind of open heavy drinking found in a nearby port town.

In relation to alcohol education he stressed it was essential to move away from the stereotype of the 'down and out' drinker. Education was needed to persuade the general public that many different types of people had drinking problems. The situation needed to be created in which people felt able to admit to a drink problem without the fear of stigma.

(b)   Senior NHS staff and health authority members

A senior clinical psychologist was visited because of his interest in alcohol related issues. He had been on a Key Tutor training course and was a member of the working party that had produced the proposal for a multi disciplinary team to be established along the lines of a community alcohol team.

There were three psychologists in his department and each covered a geographical 'patch' in which they provided a service for all patient groups except the mentally handicapped. This psychologist received about 200 referrals a year from GPs and psychiatrists while a small number were also received from probation and the social services department. Between 11 and 20% of these would have some association with drink and he suspected that his known interest in this area attracted such referrals. The largest number of these drink related referrals came from a nearby seaside resort and port. He had not received any referrals from Cornford.

He was very critical of the services of the district health authority for those with drink related problems. There was a 'drying out' facility but this was followed by the client being 'pitched out of the unit with no follow up'. For this reason he was an enthusiastic member of the working party which had proposed the establishment of some form of community alcohol team. As already indicated, the report of the working party argued that some 2,000 to 2,500 people in the district health authority had severe drinking problems and that 10,000 to 11,000 people were affected by alcohol related problems. The proposed new team was based on the principle of inter-professional working and had a strong community based focus. The difficulty would be finding sufficient finance.

He also believed there was a major need to expand alcohol education. He had a particular interest in <u>Drinkwatch</u> groups although he realised that they were difficult to establish. More generally, he wished to see primary care workers such as GPs and health visitors being made much more aware of alcohol related issues. The idea that one had to be a specialist to deal with such problems had to be broken down. Such a development would erode the stigma involved in asking for help with alcohol related problems.

The senior consultant physician at the main general hospital in Cornford was also the vice-president of the Executive Committee of the Council on Alcoholism. He was persuaded to join by the consultant psychiatrist who had done so much to argue the case for improved services. He said that the Council now had more acceptance from the health authority but that several health authority members did not believe that alcohol was an important subject for strategic planning. As a result, 'alcohol was dragging at the back of the list of priorities'. The argument for more resources had to be based on more facts and this required scrupulous research. The Council on Alcoholism also suffered from a tendency to talk rather than act.

He said that alcohol usually presented as a complication of other illnesses within acute medicine and that this might occur in 10% of cases in this health authority district. The 'classic alcoholic' was rare in the district but in any case they had a less than 5% save rate. When drink problems became chronic it was usually too late to save the patient. However, the potential problem drinker is not ill and does not present as ill; it was difficult to pick up and tackle his/her needs before it was too late.

Consultants provided a reasonable service for problem drinkers that entered hospital but there was no follow up on discharge. As a result, there was only 'a holding operation' available. Treating alcoholics was not rewarding for doctors because of the low success rate and the capacity of the patient to be 'boring' about his or her problems. GPs referred patients to AA or the Council on Alcoholism unless they needed 'drying out'. Few GPs had any real interest in the area and some wanted nothing to do with alcohol problems whatsoever.

This consultant did not have an objective view of drinking patterns. His clinical notes represented a 'peculiar' sample and his views had to be subjective. He described Cornford as "a sober little town" in which there was little overt drunkenness. He speculated that this was because of what he called "conditioned moderate social drinking". The local brewery was very careful to discourage its workers from harmful patterns of drinking. He suspected that cider drinking was an important local factor because of the large number of small scale scrumpy producers, many of which were legal but some of which were not. He felt able to pinpoint three main 'at risk' groups. The first was the 'nouveau riche' who had done well in technical jobs and had a high disposable income. The second was the poorer working class and the third was "a varied and motley group who desperately hide their drinking".

He argued that the alcoholic had already declined the educative approach. It was essential to develop more effective prevention and the main investment should be in the education of young people. Alcohol education materials for teenagers were weak and 'woolly' compared to anti-smoking materials. Alcohol education should explain to young people what represented a sensible alcohol intake. It should emphasise that moderate drinking was normal and associated with having a good time. Such education should be offered as a formal school subject which was well presented and hard hitting. The anti-smoking campaign provided a useful model although the message was different (ie moderate drinking as opposed to no smoking).

Overall, alcohol did not feature as a discussion topic among the local doctors. Alcoholism and drunkenness were not visible problems in the area and so it was doubtful if the health authority could be persuaded to make it an issue of central concern.

The chairman of the district health authority confirmed that until recently alcohol related health problems had not had a formal place in the policies of the authority. The primary reason for this was that the size of the problem within the district had not been demonstrated to the satisfaction of the medical advisers to the authority. Assertions about the nature and size of the problem had been made but there had never been any real evidence. This meant that proposals could be blocked by those who were not convinced of the importance of work in this area. He was under the impression that this attitude had been shared by the social services department.

Further money for alcohol services could not be obtained by giving this area a higher priority than service development in other areas where the need was more clearly identified. There were, for example, large waiting lists for many hospital operations and treatment including heart disease and hip replacement. The size and importance of the alcohol problem needed to be balanced against the volume of medical needs in these other areas. Evidence from the Council on Alcoholism had not been sufficiently well grounded to enable this to happen.

The chairman explained that he had a strong personal commitment to health promotion. He had encouraged his health education officers to avoid having their time dominated by one off sessions in schools. It was much more important to teach the teachers how to develop effective health education for their pupils. A health survey had been initiated which would provide a profile of the district in terms of health attitudes and behaviour. Priorities for health education officers would flow from this. Their present priority was coronary heart disease and there was no possibility that they could provide all the necessary alcohol education for the various professionals in the health authority and the local authority.

Despite the above comments, he stressed that the health authority had offered limited financial support for the development of alcohol treatment and education services but there had been a strong preference for joint finance to be used for this purpose since it would represent a combined commitment by both the health and social services authorities. Moreover, support from central government was only possible if both authorities had made a financial contribution to a locally based Council on Alcoholism.

The social services department was now much more involved in alcohol related problems and the joint finance scheme had been seen by both the health authority and the local authority as an opportunity to gain access to funds which were not easily available through their normal budgets. For example, the social services department was not in a position to shift existing funds to tackle alcohol related problems because it was struggling to meet its legal responsibilities.

As far as he could recall, the regional health authority had not identified alcohol related matters as a priority area for district health authorities.

An important factor in bringing about a change in national and regional priorities would be the willingness of the medical profession to put pressure on central government and especially the DHSS about the lack of effective action on alcohol problems.

(c) Health education

The health promotion unit in the district health authority contains a district health promotion officer and a senior health promotion officer. The unit also has one technician and shares the cost of a design studio with a neighbouring district health authority. When it was an area service, the health education unit had put undue emphasis on display generally and work in schools, to the detriment of other important issues. However, policies and priorities were reviewed in 1982 and it was agreed to develop a broader health promotion role in the community. This decision led to the setting up of a District Health Development Group, the aims of which were:

(i)   to raise the status of health promotion

(ii)   to set aims and objectives for health promotion.

The development group had a wide membership of largely senior officers. The group was able to meet only infrequently and so an executive group was formed. This was composed of the district medical officer of health, the district nursing officer, the specialist in community medicine and the district health promotion officer. The priorities for health promotion chosen by this executive group were the reduction of arterial disease and reduction of illness in elderly people. First initiatives in line with these priorities were promotion of a non-smoking campaign, a health survey to establish positive health indices, and a detailed survey of the problems of elderly people in one community.

At the time of writing the results of the health promotion survey had not been produced. The survey questionnaire was distributed to 1,000 adults aged between 15 and 64 in each of four general practices in the district and to a thousand employees of the health authority. The response rate overall was in the region of 65%. Difficulties were experienced in coding and analysing the responses, but it was planned to present the results to a meeting of the health authority late in 1985. Drinking habits and attitudes towards alcohol were included among the questions posed in the survey.

The district health education officer expected the survey would show that the volume of alcohol problems had been overestimated in the various 'guesstimates' and in the local press. He had no firm information on drinking patterns apart from the survey but he perceived the Cornford area as being largely composed of moderate drinkers. He suspected there might be more of a problem amongst young people under 30, especially if they were cider drinkers. Neither the health promotion group nor the health promotion planning group had identified alcohol as a priority issue. Most senior doctors did not believe there was a large alcohol misuse problem in the local population.

He believed alcohol education should concentrate primarily on working with young people. Teachers needed training and he hoped that Key Tutors who had been on the Drinking Choices course might be able to play a lead role in this. The 'agency' that led such training might be the Council on Alcoholism, the health promotion unit or the local education authority. Health education was a priority within the LEA but was not always recognised as such at school level. This situation might be remedied by the appointment of a full time health education adviser.

He explained that senior staff in the health authority and local authority tended to stay in their authorities for a long time and there was a strong social network amongst these officers that aided inter-professional working. The primary focus for alcohol related questions - including education - was seen as the Council on Alcoholism. He saw the priorities of the Council as being to provide counselling services, to disseminate information and to co-operate with the health promotion unit. He said it remained unclear whether the proposed Department of Alcoholism would shift the focus of the alcohol network from the Council on Alcoholism to the health service.

At the time of interview, the senior health promotion officer had been spending some time on supporting the Great British Fun Run. Longer term commitments included responsibility for the resources of the unit and their appropriate use, together with other aspects of information provision. Thus, he was trying to work more closely with nursing staff who worked in the community, as their role in health education was of particular importance and they made extensive use of the services of the unit. In connection with this he felt there was a need for antenatal education to make people more aware of the links between alcohol consumption in pregnancy and foetal alcohol syndrome.

Another important area of activity for this officer was schools liaison. He confirmed that alcohol education had not emerged as a priority area or major topic of discussion within the local education authority. However, he had arranged for the Tacade director to give a presentation to local teachers on their alcohol education syllabus.[5] He said that in other health issues such as coronary heart disease, there were clear data and clear recommendations. The situation was far more vague and unclear in the area of alcohol education.

Alcohol education took place in schools in the context of an overall health education syllabus. Most secondary schools acknowledged the need for 'education for life'. Higher rates of unemployment had reinforced the importance of teaching life and social skills. Health education should be undertaken throughout primary and secondary schools and it should not be crisis orientated. If some pupils were seen going to a public house at lunchtime, a lecture on the evils of drink was likely to have limited effect and might be counter-productive. Health education and alcohol education needed to explore attitudes and feelings rather than just impart factual information. The health promotion unit could help schools in the planning of their health education syllabus, and this might include directing them to alcohol education material produced by the Health Education Council, Tacade, etc. However, health education was poorly developed in the local education authority and this needed to be tackled through the appointment of a health education adviser. At the moment, health education was 'tagged on' to the job description of the adviser with responsibility for home economics and needlework.

He said he was unsure about the nature of local drinking problems although he was certain they impacted upon more people than illegal drugs or solvents. He wanted to wait for results from the health promotion survey, although a field trial of 100 had found hardly anyone who claimed to drink five or more times per week. He thought low unemployment might mean there were less alcohol problems than in many areas of Britain. He had been on a Key Tutor course but he would wait until the survey results before deciding how involved to become in alcohol education. However, the South West alcohol education programme was helping to shift priorities and make it easier for him to justify the allocation of time to alcohol education.

(d)   School of nursing

A psychiatric nurse tutor who had been on a Key Tutor course was visited.   He had three main responsibilities, namely registered mental nurses (RMNs), enrolled mental nurses and registered general nurses.   He was involved with continuing as well as professional education for these groups.

In his own training as a nurse, he had been taught that high alcohol consumption was related to deviant personalities.   However, he began to realise that his own drinking patterns and those of his colleagues were affecting work performance.   They were not psychopaths, and so he realised it was necessary to reject most of what he had been taught.   However, this process of discovery led him to develop a specialist interest in alcohol and drug abuse which was reflected in his present teaching activities.   He was developing a three phase package on alcohol related issues for RMNs and enrolled nurses.

The first phase looked at definitions and eradicated the term 'alcoholism'.   He compared student stereotypes of the 'wino' and 'down and outs' with more middle class examples of excessive drinking.   He went on to ask students about the place of alcohol in their own lives and how this changed over time.   They looked at strategies for sensible drinking.   The HEC pamphlet That's the limit was used and students were encouraged to keep diaries on what they drank and how much it cost.   Students were asked why they drank and the benefits they felt they obtained.   This was compared with the dangers of alcohol and the signs of existence of a drink problem.   The students were asked if they had ever experienced a blackout from drink.   Did they drink to reduce anxiety or stress at work?   He believed self awareness teaching was essential for the student who might fall apart and resort to alcohol because of a new job, a new career and new relationships.

The second phase focused more specifically on the patient.   He argued to the nurses that assessment for all patients should include a consideration of their drinking patterns.   The aim was to achieve recognition of a drinking problem before it was too late to help. Students were taught about what helping agencies were available for those who did have such a drinking problem.   He preferred the open philosophy of the Council on Alcoholism to the moralistic and secretive approach of AA.   The third phase of his teaching was most applicable to RMNs.   This looked at their potential active involvement in counselling, group work, detoxification, treatment

(Antabuse etc), rehabilitation, social skills training, relaxation training and assertion training.

(e)   Primary health care

Two doctors, a trainee GP, a health visitor and a community psychiatric nurse were seen together at the GP practice in Cornford that was most frequently mentioned for its willingness to help patients with alcohol related problems. The two GPs stressed that alcohol was an issue with three types of patient. First, there were patients with a declared drinking problem. Second, there were heavy drinkers who suffered from problems of psychological stress. Third, there were patients with physical illnesses in which alcohol played a part. They agreed that they missed most of the last group and that they only picked up a proportion from the other two groups. They felt there was little incentive for them to improve their efficiency since treatment facilities were so limited. This blockage meant they made little effort to uncover drink related problems. They could refer people to be 'dried out' but then there was little preventive follow up.

The GPs explained that different GPs had different approaches to treatment. Some insisted on abstinence along the lines of AA. Some took a flexible view along the lines of the Council on Alcoholism. The GPs at this practice tried to offer their own counselling although they did refer people to the specialist agencies. They had team discussions about the needs of patients and this often led to the involvement of the community psychiatric nurse. This nurse explained that she had a caseload of 44 and that 10% of these were alcoholic and a further 20% were alcohol related. The real difficulty was those patients who failed to respond to treatment and counselling; medical staff from outside the practice often failed to offer help and this left the GP practice with an intractable and time consuming problem.

A list of possible groups 'at risk' in the Cornford area was supplied. This included the upwardly mobile who had moved from a trade to a profession, the council house tenant, the wives of farmers and the single homeless parent. An inability to cope with the stress of normal life was seen as a frequent factor. Home brewing and cider drinking were seen as problematic features of local life.

They also agreed that they were little involved in alcohol education beyond one to one counselling about the dangers of drink. The advertising revenue of the drinks industry was enormous; the advertisers should be made or persuaded to say that drink only offered the good life if taken in small amounts. This required dogmatic statements about what represented the danger zone for alcohol consumption. People needed to be made to realise how their units of consumption added up during the day and placed their health 'at risk', even though they were never drunk. They needed to be presented with a catalogue about the destructiveness of alcohol in terms of its role in divorce, work accidents, child abuse and other social problems.

Counselling services and alcohol education

(a)   Statutory agencies

Discussions were held with four staff of the social services department and three members of the probation service. The social workers included the assistant director for mental health social work in the county. It also included the area director and deputy area director for hospital social work. Hospital social workers were split into three teams, namely child health and family guidance, acute and elderly services, and the psychiatric team. The team leader of psychiatric social workers was also interviewed. This last social worker wished to go on a Key Tutor course.

Three of these officers emphasised that alcohol related problems were a low priority for the social services department and that such problems were not very common in their community. One of them, for example, explained that the district health authority had been pressurising the social services department to become more involved but the view of social services remained that service development for such groups as children 'at risk' and the frail elderly remained a much higher priority. They were sceptical about the justification for having a social worker in any new Department of Alcoholism since they argued there were far too few referrals to justify such an investment of scarce resources. They felt that those interested in alcohol related problems had failed to demonstrate the size of the problem in the Cornford area. Such doubts made it much more sensible to support a modest grant to the Council on Alcoholism since the statutory agencies could not continue to take on more and more responsibilites.

The officers found it difficult to specify any particular drinking problems in the Cornford area. The population of Cornford was seen as stable and the level of social control from local residents was high. The social services department dealt mainly with 'problem families' and the bulk of family violence was not alcohol related. Most misfits in the community conformed or left for areas where they were not known. This made it very difficult for people to admit they had an alcohol problem. Excessive drinking was often hidden and sufferers would refer themselves to secret groups like AA. There was rarely any public drunkenness or violence in public houses. The area director differed slightly in that he felt the county would be no different from the rest of the country in its drinking patterns and that young people were especially 'at risk'; it was just that alcohol related referrals did not trickle through to the social services department.

The team leader for psychiatric social workers had a different perspective. He had forwarded his name to go on a Key Tutor course and he was a member of the working party that had proposed a Department of Alcoholism. He stressed it was important to consider more than just the needs of the 'chronic' alcoholic who needed support after 'drying out'. Alcohol abuse was a major factor in many cases of domestic violence. He believed that 33% of the clients of his social workers suffered from consequences of alcohol abuse. Education was needed to bring 'alcoholism out of the cupboard' so that people felt able to approach Drinkwatch groups before they developed chronic problems.

A senior probation officer was interviewed as were two probation officers based at Cornford prison. The senior probation officer was responsible for seven probation officers. They received 50 to 60 new cases per year and had about 160 cases 'on the books' at any one time. The majority of these referrals were for criminal convictions (85%) while the remainder were from the Divorce Court when it was not satisfied with the arrangements made for children. The minimum probation order lasted for six months, and on average it was 18 months. Every person on a criminal charge had to have a social enquiry report and this was 250 cases per year.

He said it was difficult to set a percentage for alcohol related cases because many offenders used drink in an attempt to excuse their crime. It was very difficult to know when this was the truth. Problems with drink were common in divorce cases. There was a recognisable group of regular petty offenders who had a major drink problem. If an offender admitted to a drink problem, the probation officer would arrange help through the GP or an AA group. Women often turned to drink when under the stress of a divorce case. If they were referred to the GP, they tended to be prescribed drugs that were just as addictive.

However, he believed that alcohol was not a serious problem around Cornford where the drinking was 'pretty average'. Cornford was a stable community with little social isolation. People helped each other and so there was little need to turn to drink. The public houses in Cornford were an important part of social life but most focused on serving couples and providing food rather than encouraging binge drinking from single sex groups. Adolescents were probably most 'at risk' because of the number of clubs and discos with late licences. He said that alcohol education would not stop people drinking because it was part of normal social life. The emphasis should be not on what excessive drinking did to the individual but rather its impact upon the rest of the family.

The senior probation officer at the prison was a member of the Executive Committee of the Council on Alcoholism. He explained that both he and his colleague offered support to inmates in the prison and also assisted them in preparing for release. Prisoners had to face the reality of their disadvantage when they left prison. One disadvantage was the tendency of many to drift into heavy drinking. This was especially true of persistent petty offenders who were often homeless single people with not many ties. Many of these people had little real involvement with this part of the county, many came from the nearby seaside conurbation, while others were just passing through the county. At present, there were 140 convicted people in the prison and he suspected that up to 100 of them were in for offences that were drink related. Only about two of these were likely to be Cornford residents.

Both he and his colleague said that inmates were surprised to find that five to eight pints per night was not seen as normal social drinking. Such people often had few other interests. The public house was the focus of their social life. It was therefore difficult to tackle drink as an issue with the inmates especially since sentences were often for short periods. The prisoners denied there was anything wrong with their drinking patterns, whereas they might accept that other aspects of their life, such as heavy gambling, was a factor in their law breaking. Despite these obstacles the probation officers wanted to develop courses on alcoholism with the help of the Council on Alcoholism.

They both believed that social workers and probation officers received inadequate training about alcohol related issues. One of them supplied the only alcohol input into his own professional training, as a result of a placement working with vagrant alcoholics. There was a wrong assumption that everyone knows about alcohol and so it was not addressed properly in professional courses. However, people working with those with drinking problems have to be aware of the physical and emotional implications of coming off drink. Such professionals also needed to educate people that the consumption of six or seven pints per night represented excessive drinking. Alcohol education needed to be offered to all young people in schools and youth clubs. The senior probation officer concluded the discussion by stating that both military families and members of the farming community often had drinking problems in the local community but that these problems were usually kept hidden.

(b)   Voluntary agencies

A volunteer counsellor for the Samaritans said that the service in the county had 90 volunteer counsellors and these dealt with 1,473 new callers in 1984. Many of these callers were 'regulars' who appreciated periodic telephone contact with the Samaritans. About a quarter of the calls were about personal relationships from people who cannot relate to others. The Samaritans encouraged them to join local societies or self help groups.

22 of the callers specified that their central problem was excessive drinking. Another 15 were the wives or relatives of problem drinkers. The numbers in this category were, therefore, very small although drink was often a factor in cases where the main concern was domestic violence or marital squabbles. Most problem drinkers know of both AA and the Council on Alcoholism. They usually want to contact AA but need some encouragement. The Council on Alcoholism was not used for referral because it lacked a network of volunteer counsellors. About half the fifteen relatives were referred to Al Anon; the rest were satisfied with the chance to talk over their problems. She stressed there was no role for the Samaritans in alcohol education. They were passive and provided an opportunity for troubles to be shared. They did not give advice about appropriate behaviour and lifestyle. The personal view of the respondent was that alcohol related problems could only be reduced by restrictions on advertising and the reduction of outlets. A terrific upsurge in consumption began when supermarkets were allowed to sell alcohol. A housewife could now buy drink with her shopping without anyone knowing; the lonely middle aged housewife was often tempted to drink on her own in the afternoon.

The vice-chairman of the Marriage Guidance Council had contacted the Dorset network of counsellors and asked them about the number of cases in which alcohol was the primary problem. The consensus was that this number was exceedingly small. However, alcohol was seen as being a partial factor in about 25% of cases although she stressed the extent to which this was a rough and ready judgement.

She defined an alcohol problem as occurring when the health, efficiency, competence and personal relationships of an individual were affected by drinking. If a case included a severe alcohol problem, AA or Al Anon could be contacted. She was the representative of the Marriage Guidance Council on the Council on Alcoholism but this was a relatively new organisation and not yet used for referrals. However, it was unusual for clients to be referred on to such agencies since it was demoralising to be 'shunted off' somewhere else. The emphasis of their work was upon enabling the clients to make their own decisions about how to resolve their own problems rather than to insist upon a particular course of action.

The vice-chairman thought that alcohol education was of little interest to her counsellors. There was the problem of long distances and the counsellors already had regular commitments with fortnightly case discussions and meetings with tutors. They had to return to the national training centre in Rugby every four years. Her counsellors expressed surprise that they were being asked a specific question about the importance of alcohol problems. They felt that as part of their training, they learnt that anything that came up might have to be addressed in their counselling. The vice-chairman was certain that these counsellors would have been told about the signs and symptoms of excessive drinking in their training. Observation was part of the training. The counsellors did not perceive alcohol problems as an issue requiring further expertise and knowledge.

(c)   The churches

A Baptist minister was contacted who ran a youth club in Cornford for 14 to 20 year olds on a Friday evening. About 100 to 150 young people turned up for each session. He also ran a more distinctly Christian group of 14 to 19 year olds on a Sunday night that attracted up to 40 young people. He was concerned about the lack of social facilities for older teenagers in the Cornford area. Their social networks were disrupted when friends left for university.

Those who remained felt frustrated by reduced job opportunities and poor social facilities. The teenagers involved with the Baptist church nearly all came from professional families and he stressed that he had little contact with teenagers from the council estate.

This minister had previously worked in isolated rural areas such as Dartmoor rather than a market town. In the former, under age drinking in public houses was widespread and socially accepted. In Cornford, parents had very strict moral standards and such behaviour was often frowned upon. He believed Cornford had fewer drinking problems than the rural areas but that it did still have a drinking problem, especially among young people, many of whom were secret drinkers. He said that groups of 16 and 17 year olds held parties at home and got drunk. He believed that about seven of his 200 youth club members were in danger of becoming dependent on alcohol. In 1984, he visited over 30 teenagers at home because he thought they had a drink problem. These youngsters all consumed up to three or four pints a day or the equivalent. Two thirds of these cases involved boys and one third were girls. He estimated that half had reduced their drinking as a result of his intervention, which focused on explaining the facts about alcohol and stressing that they had the capacity to make their own choice about levels of consumption. He believed most teenage drink problems stemmed from the failure to channel energies into constructive pastimes; there were just not enough interesting things for young people to do in Cornford. Young people also felt that drinking was a sign of maturity. It was difficult to place these social problems on a public agenda because Cornford residents liked to pretend that everything in their community was above reproach.

He argued that it was essential that alcohol education should be offered in an effective way to all young people in middle and senior schools. Such education had to be participative by allowing young people to contribute their own views. Teachers needed to treat the pupils as individuals who had choices. However, he believed secondary schools in Cornford were often weak at this type of teaching. The tendency was often to 'talk down' to pupils and this resulted in a failure to engage their interest.

Alcohol and the education department

(a) The schools

The home economics adviser for the education department had agreed to take on responsibility for health education about twelve months previously. The attempt to establish a health education adviser post with joint finance money from the Area Health Authority and Local Education Authority had not, so far, been successful. The home economics adviser stressed that the present arrangement was not very satisfactory; she had responsibility for parentcraft, needlecraft, home economics and middle school health education. Health education was only a quarter of her brief and alcohol education was only a small part of that. Despite these problems, she was going to find time to go on a Key Tutor course.

The education authority had recently produced curriculum statements for most subjects including personal and social education. This stressed the importance of teaching social skills while assessment and profiling were also major new developments. Each school was being asked to assess its curriculum against the county statement and make a response. This process would enable the home economics adviser to obtain a clearer overall view about the quality and depth of health education in county schools. Each school was autonomous and it was difficult for her to encourage a more consistent approach with such limited time available. Some schools did not even have a written curriculum for health education and in general it was not seen as a high priority area. She stressed that advisers had no brief to intervene in curriculum matters in individual schools. They could only advise when requested to do so by the head, a teacher or a senior colleague.

The county had been chosen as a pilot area for the My body[6] project. Unfortunately, alcohol had been omitted from consideration, which was a mistake. The parentcraft syllabus did address alcohol issues because of the foetal alcohol syndrome. Teachers who had watched the video giving information about this were amazed and horrified. She said that the director of Tacade was often used for in-service drugs and alcohol education for teachers in the county.[7] She was uncertain about the best approach to alcohol education although she was convinced shock tactics were wrong because they had undesirable side-effects such as 'whisper campaigns'. Headteachers were the crucial factor in whether or not alcohol education was developed in local schools.

Four headteachers and one teacher responsible for health education were visited   The headteacher of a middle school explained that he had 550 boys and girls and that 12% of these were from a professional background, 30% from a white collar/private housing estate, 30% from council estates and 28% from small rural villages.   He said that the school had a clear written health education programme that lasted throughout the four years and tried to build up themes and concepts.   The nine year olds started with the self and the thirteen year olds ended with a consideration of the need for social responsibility.   The school used the Think well[8] materials that had been produced by the School Councils Project. Alcohol was addressed with smoking under the title of 'Deadly decisions'. 'Deadly decisions' was part of the last term of the fourth year in which pupils were asked to consider decisions that they will soon have to make. There was a heavy emphasis upon class and group discussions. Health education was not an examinable subject and this was a great pity because it reduced its status. However, the centrality of this subject needed to be increased because most young people receive little or no health education from their parents.

The headteacher of the other middle school said he had 410 pupils between nine and 13 years and that there were slightly more boys than girls. Their main catchment area was well established private housing estates and certain rural villages; parents were largely professional people. The headteacher had been in post for only one year and prior to his arrival, health education was split between two physical education teachers.   The senior health education officer from the district health authority had helped them develop an integrated health education curriculum that would be a formal part of the school programme throughout the four years. Alcohol could be addressed in the fourth year through the Think well 'Deadly decisions' material.   However, the headteacher did not believe there was an alcohol problem among his thirteen year olds, and so there was much more concentration upon smoking. Overall, most emphasis was placed on road safety because more children were killed on the road than by drugs or alcohol.

Staff were apprehensive about the new curriculum because they were wary of sensitive subjects. The health promotion unit of the health authority ran a course for staff in the school. The new curriculum was launched with a parents' evening and this attracted over one hundred parents. He felt they were still learning about how to develop effective health education teaching. However, he was certain that it was a mistake to rely on guest speakers who were experts on social problems such as glue sniffing since this only encouraged more interest in the problem behaviour and the desire to experiment.

The headteacher of the boys' senior school said he had 760 pupils including 160 in the sixth form. Until five years ago it was a grammar school for boys. He expressed dissatisfaction with health education in the school. He had inherited a school two and a half years ago that approached every subject in a very traditional manner. All the school curricula were still under review. Alcohol education was part of the science programme given to 13 year olds. A variety of health education subjects including sex education were introduced as part of both a broad science education programme and also within religious studies. Alcohol was addressed under abuse of drugs which looked at how this was associated with mental and emotional problems. The teacher responsible for the co-ordination of the health education syllabus later explained that health education represented one third of the biology course during this year. Some health education issues might be tackled in biology lessons in later years but not all pupils took this subject. Religious studies was a person centred curriculum, and so it was difficult to specify the extent to which health education issues were addressed. Both teachers agreed it was difficult to know exactly what health education was received by which pupils; the situation was even less co-ordinated when the varying inputs on health education from their three feeder middle schools were considered.

The headteacher of the senior school for girls said she had 700 pupils including a sixth form of 150. Pupils were organised into 'houses' and the head of each house was responsible for what was called personal and social education. This was offered for one period a week in the third year and for two periods in the fourth and fifth years. Personal and social education issues were also addressed through assembly, tutorial groups, social biology, religious studies and parentcraft classes. However, the health education element of all this was often very limited and would vary from house to house and according to the options chosen by the pupils. Personal and social education sessions tended to be dominated by careers advice and moral education issues. Religious studies had a wide focus and also addressed moral education issues. She knew this did include drug abuse and alcoholism because it was part of the examination syllabus.

These teachers varied in their perception of drinking patterns and problems in the Cornford area and how this related to under age drinking. The middle school teachers stressed that discipline was not a problem and that there were relatively few social problems in their school. The children were too young to be very much 'at risk' from alcohol consumption, although the odd incident might occur. One teacher stressed how his school was under enormous pressure to achieve academic success while the other perceived his pupils' parents as less demanding in that respect. Cornford was discussed as a community with little social deprivation, high employment and no ethnic minority problems. Parents could be depended upon to support the school when teachers 'jumped on' bad behaviour. The teachers from the senior schools and also an educational welfare officer were slightly less complacent. Their schools had no major problem, especially compared with other parts of the country, but there was a recognition of the existence of under age drinking. There was a concern that the academically less motivated might be tempted to abuse drink and that this might worsen as a problem if employment and career prospects worsened. Reference was also made to the lack of social facilities for young people in Cornford and the surrounding villages. The education welfare officer said that many young people do use public houses in Cornford, but that this problem was far greater in the seaside towns of the county.

(b)   The youth service

The youth training officer for the district said that there were probably up to 1,500 adults working or volunteering in youth organisations in the county. There were 48 full time youth workers and he organised an extensive in-service programme, including four full day sessions for this group. He was responsible for a seven month course for 70 part time youth leaders, an introductory course for potential youth workers and an advanced course for another 20 which was based on four residential weekends. He did send materials on alcohol to youth leaders, such as the Tacade alcohol education card game and the 20 minute BBC video on Booze. However, his training courses did not specifically isolate alcohol as a subject in its own right but as part of a wider range of areas under the heading of 'Risk areas for young people'. Other agencies had been involved including the director of Tacade and personnel from Area Health Education. It was felt that education within the youth service was of a more informal and personal nature, and that the more formalised style was probably being covered within schools. The focus of the adult leader courses was related to intervention skills and the development of support and counselling.

47

He said that Cornford teenagers could be split up into three main groups. The teenagers with more access to funds were attracted to licensed premises for their 'aura' of adulthood. These might be public houses or often one of the local clubs where groups and disco music were an added attraction. Youth clubs attracted a wider range of young people but did not have a great number of members from the 'professional classes' due to homework or specialist activity participation. However, some of the most disruptive youngsters were not interested in youth clubs and they were often banned from public houses because they were too 'scruffy'. This group tended to roam the streets and they often got into trouble. The biggest problem with teenage drinking in pubs and social clubs was the large round which encouraged everyone to drink to excess.[9] Young people would ignore a completely anti-drink message but they might be persuaded to place less emphasis upon the 'round' as the main mechanism for buying their drink.

In the Cornford area, adults from the professional classes joined certain clubs and frequented certain public houses. These could normally be visited only by car and this reduced drinking. Working men drank much nearer home and visited their pubs on foot. Many were involved in skittles, darts and crib leagues. Men might be out five or six times per week and alcohol consumption was the norm. When driving to 'away' fixtures the burden of driving was usually taken in rota thus allowing the remainder to consume at will. Many young people saw these 'sporting activities' and their settings as the acceptable life for men in the area and often were invited to participate at a comparatively young age.

A full time youth leader ran a centre in Cornford that was open five nights per week and Sunday afternoons for young people aged between 12 and 21. He said that the majority of the 70 attenders per night were 16 or over of which about 65% were boys. Most of the users were from 'blue collar' homes on the main council estates. The children of professional parents often go somewhere more 'constructive' than the youth centre.

He said he took a very hard line on drinking at his centre. Only soft drinks were sold at discos and he refused entry to 'rowdy youths' that had already been consuming alcohol. Drink problems still arose at the centre but far less frequently than when he arrived five years ago. He still had to take bottles from members and 'strange' bottles were still found in the toilets. However, alcohol consumption by club members had been reduced although this might be because he had discouraged heavy drinkers from attending. He ran a social education group on Monday nights and this underlined how often drink was a precursor to getting into all kinds of difficulties. His club had posters on alcohol education which were provided by the National Association of Youth Clubs. Good materials on the dangers of drink were difficult to obtain.

He believed young people started to drink in pubs because they were attracted by the adult environment and they wanted to get out of their own homes. There was nowhere else to go in Cornford. He had run discos in the premises of a plush local commercial disco with a soft drinks bar and this attracted up to 300 young people. He was especially concerned about young people when they first received a wage, even if this was only a YTS trainee allowance. This group had few financial obligations and a great deal of their money often went on alcohol. Such people needed to be taught while still at school that alcohol can easily become addictive and that it does impair judgement.

Alcohol and the law

(a)   The police

Three police officers were contacted, namely the chief inspector in the community relations department of the police authority, an inspector based in Cornford and a police constable who was a juvenile liaison officer. The police authority was split into Eastern, Central and Western Divisions, and the latter division covered Cornford. It was explained that statistics were available for three types of alcohol related offences, namely drunk and incapable, drunk and disorderly and drink and driving. However, alcohol was a factor in many other types of crime, including criminal damage. The statistics for drink and drive offences are presented in Table 4.

Table 4:   Roadside breathtests in the Cornford police area

	Tests required	Positive	Negative	Failure to provide	Precluded by hospital
1981	2,494	771	1,597	118	8
1982	3,083	872	2,058	152	1
1983	4,031	1,117	2,647	262	5
1984	3,754	1,138	2,244	366	6

Statistical information on the other two offences was slightly less clearcut. Prior to December 1981, 'simple drunks' (ie the drunk and incapable) were arrested, detained until sober, charged and brought to court. However, this was the first police authority to instigate a cautioning policy for this category of offence. People in this group were still arrested and detained until sober. However, a charge sheet was then filled out, they were cautioned and then released. This saved time and kept alcoholics out of prison. In 1984, 71 of the 309 cautioned were from the Western Division as were 44 of the 209 court appearances. The biggest problem area was the main seaside conurbation where there was a large group of 'winos'.

Table 5:   Cautions and court appearances for 'simple drunks' and the drunk and disorderly

Year	Cautioned ('Simple drunks')	Court appearance (Drunk & disorderly)
1982	388	339
1983	277	238
1984	309	209

It was also possible to obtain some data for these offences from the Cornford sub-division. This sub-division had given cautions to ten 'simple drunks' in 1983 and to eight in 1984. 502 individuals were taken to court and this included 69 alcohol related offences, as can be seen from Table 6.

Table 6:   Alcohol related offences in the Cornford sub division,
            1983 and 1984

Offence	Total	Cornford residents	Men	Women
Drunken driving (Positive breath test)	59	27	55	4
Drunk & disorderly	10	7	10	Nil
Licensing infringement	None taken to court in 1984. Couple of prosecutions in 1983.			
Under age drinking	None taken to court: but juvenile drinking exists			

Some information about the alcohol involvement of juveniles was
supplied.   Since 1984 a breakdown for this category had been
introduced for juvenile cautions. In 1984 the police authority made
1,714 cautions and 73 of these were for alcohol involvement by
juveniles, including 23 from the Western Division.   These police
officers felt some concern at the growth of teenage and under age
drinking and they felt this was linked to the growth in outlets. One
of them was particularly worried about 'low ability' and 'high
ability' children.   The first were often completely alcohol
orientated.   The second group had easy access to alcohol at home
and their problems were often 'hidden'.   However, the general
consensus was that drinking problems in the county were only
'average' and that they were less than average in the Cornford
area.   They did not believe that the police had a role to play in
alcohol education.   The police were concerned with offences and
there were many other issues that had to be prioritised. However,
the police wished to be compassionate and they wanted to
encourage offenders who drank heavily to approach AA or the new
network of counsellors from the Council on Alcoholism.

(b)   Magistrates

The three magistrates with whom discussions were held did not
express great concern about the extent of alcohol related offences
coming before their bench.   Drunken driving offences were not
particularly high. The middle classes were now very worried about
losing their licences. The police had raised the issue of under age

drinking and this had been discussed by their juvenile panel at a meeting addressed by the local consultant psychiatrist and the senior counsellor from the Council on Alcoholism. The extent of under age drinking, however, seemed to have reduced over the last twelve months. Minor criminal damage and petty theft was often explained by the defendant in terms of reduced judgement as a result of excessive drinking. However, magistrates usually felt this did not represent a valid excuse. Their most worrying problem was the 'old lag' who was a hardened alcoholic. It was very difficult to help them but their numbers were decreasing. Excessive drinking was controlled in village communities through the process of informal social control. A village was very different from an anonymous town or city. Cornford and district was a law abiding community.

Licensing powers were unclear over a number of issues such as what was meant by a special occasional licence. This might be asked for by a village football team for eight home games. They try to be consistent so as to avoid embarrassment. It was difficult to turn down licence applications because their concession was not dependent upon the applicant being able to prove a need for further outlets. It could only be refused if the premises were seen as inappropriate. They had little discretion on most licensing matters and they sometimes wondered why applications had to be made when the licences had to be granted.

Alcohol education in Cornford and the South West programme

Respondents were interviewed before the Cornford Briefing Conference in June 1985 and 14 of them were already aware of the existence of the South West alcohol education programme (see Table 7). This group consisted mainly of those associated with the Council on Alcoholism.

Respondents in this locality study were different from those in the other three studies in terms of their enthusiasm for the South West programme. The following three chapters will show that the Councils on Alcoholism in the other areas expressed concern that their expertise and previous work was not being given sufficient recognition by the Health Education Council (HEC). In Cornford, the arrival of the programme was seen as offering an important opportunity to establish the Council on Alcoholism on a much firmer footing than had been achieved previously. The opportunity of establishing a local group of Key Tutors was seen as an advantage to the Council in terms of the capacity to increase the visibility of alcohol education within the county. Elsewhere, the research team believes that proposals for local networks of Key Tutors could be seen as a threat to the autonomy, power and priorities of the Councils on Alcoholism. It will be interesting to study whether the Cornford situation remains the same when respondents are revisited. (Will there be frustration at the lack of financial support available through the HEC? Will proposals for some form of community alcohol team make the ultimate loyalty of the Key Tutor group more of a sensitive issue?) The Council on Alcoholism is attempting to establish itself on a firm financial footing. So far, the presence of the South West programme has been seen as aiding arguments for more resources. However, this may change if the future activities of Key Tutors are not seen by local resource gatekeepers as having anything to do with the Council on Alcoholism. Fortunately, the health promotion unit, the Council on Alcoholism and the Key Tutors seem aware of this danger and able to establish arrangements that are satisfactory to all sides. This may not be true of all parts of the South West.

Seven people from the area covered by the district health authority have been on Key Tutor courses and all of them were seen during the fieldwork. At the time of visiting four had completed a course and three were about to attend. All course participants were positive about their experience although some found the course over tiring while some were surprised by the lack of knowledge of some participants. However, the participant who knew least about the subject found the alcohol input excellent and essential to any ability to play an active role in future developments. All expressed an interest in forming a local network of Key Tutors although there were some reservations. The main concern was whether they could negotiate time and legitimacy from their senior managers to pursue these educational activities in a professional way. Some were worried that the public launch of the South West programme could lead to a deluge of requests for courses. One stressed that alcohol education would still have to jostle with other priorities. These Key Tutors had agreed that the initial priority group for targeting should be teachers because of the central importance of offering effective alcohol education in schools.

Table 7:   Knowledge of the South West alcohol education programme

Subject area of respondent		Number of respondents	Aware of programme	Unaware of programme
1. Alcohol and specialist provision in the voluntary sector	a) The Council on Alcoholism	3	3	–
	b) Self help groups	2	–	2
2. Alcohol and the NHS	a) Psychiatric services	2	2	–
	b) Senior NHS staff and health authority members	3	2	1
	c) Health education	2	2	–
	d) Schools of nursing	1	1	–
	e) Primary health care	5	0	5
3. Counselling services and alcohol education	a) Statutory agencies	7	3	4
	b) Voluntary agencies	2	–	2
	c) The churches	1	–	1
4. Alcohol and the education department	a) The schools	7	1	6
	b) The youth service	2	–	2
5. Alcohol and the law	a) The police	3	–	3
	b) Magistrates	3	–	3
TOTALS		43	14	29

Drinking patterns and problems in Cornford

Many of the respondents in Cornford did not give the impression that they had a clear view of local drinking patterns and problems. It was very difficult to disentangle prejudice, anxiety and real knowledge; views were not normally backed up with reliable evidence. Statements about these drinking patterns and problems and the need for alcohol education were related in a complex way to individual attitudes to, and consumption of, drink. This was true of all four locality studies.

However, certain themes did recur in the Cornford discussions and these will now be briefly outlined. The town was characterised as a law abiding community in which there were few drinking problems. This attitude was perhaps best summed up by the respondent who said that "alcohol is not a serious problem. A fair amount of drinking goes on, but it is pretty average."

The town was often compared favourably in relation to alcohol problems to two large seaside towns in the same county. Those who wished to challenge this complacent view such as members of the Council on Alcoholism were expected to provide 'facts'. The Council on Alcoholism and the consultant psychiatrist responded by attempting to quantify the suffering caused by even 'average' rates of drinking within our society. These projections were then ignored by others on the grounds that they were speculative.

The most common group picked out as 'at risk' from alcohol abuse were young people who were seen as bored by the lack of facilities in the town while at the same time financially quite well off. References were made to under age drinking and binge drinking but respondents in the town tended to be more censorious of such behaviour than those in the next study. However, this drinking was not seen as often associated with crime and so was not a major issue in the community. Most respondents seemed to feel working class youth and communities were more at risk than the middle class who usually approached alcohol in a sensible manner. The exceptions to this were often the isolated and lonely such as some elderly people, widows and mothers 'at home'. Several references were made to the impossibility of knowing what went on in isolated rural villages that were very 'feudal'.

The most striking theme in this study was the emphasis upon the 'respectability' of the community. Troublemakers and non-conformists were frozen out and forced to leave. Informal social control was very strong. People hated social problems to be raised by professionals or in the press because this reflected badly on the name of the town. Respondents felt this would make it difficult to increase the visibility of alcohol education.

Two pieces of research may help to provide a clear picture of actual drinking practices. The first of these is the Health Promotion survey. Cornford was chosen as a locality study by the research team partly because of the survey. This should provide at least part of the answer as to the nature of drinking patterns in the Cornford community. However, the research team suspects that the debate will continue because the results will be seen as inconclusive by all sides. The other piece of work was that carried out on drinking outlets by Adrian Franklin on behalf of the research team. One of the two localities studied was Cornford and this involved both participant observation and discussions with a limited number of landlords. He concluded:

> "In terms of the amounts of alcohol consumed, the overall impression was that the majority of regular customers in pubs drink very moderately indeed. The principal object of visits to pubs is to socialise with friends and family. In Cornford ..... publicans reported a greater concern with diet and health which was reflected in a decline in the amount consumed and an increase in less alcoholic or non-intoxicating drink. Publicans also reported that individuals in youthful cohorts in more 'respectable' pubs were no longer under any pressure from peers to drink alcohol. No extra status was gained by drinking alcohol. Indeed, overt drunkenness in respectable pubs is disappearing; people who get drunk and noisy are asked to leave by the publican with the approval of his customers. Intentional heavy drinking is largely confined to a small section of the youthful, single male population, who tend to dominate the pubs they regularly use.
>
> Pubs are still very important focal points in the community, being the only communal facility in many localities. The changes that have been outlined here suggest that they are now a focus point for a greater range of social relations than they were previously."[10]

However, Franklin goes on to indicate that:

"Publicans themselves were confused about alcohol and health, and whilst many knew health could be damaged by drinking, they perpetuated many of the myths about alcohol, eg drinking spirits is more dangerous than beer, some can drink vast quantities and experience no ill health."[11]

It could be that moderate drinking to most publicans is the avoidance of overt drunkenness, violence and binge drinking. The relevance of the claimed low levels of alcohol consumed by most customers in most public houses in Cornford can only be understood in relation to drinking patterns in the home and other settings by residents, many of whom will have a high disposable income.

References

1. Franklin, A. (1985), Pub drinking and the licensed trade: a study of drinking cultures and local community in two areas of South West England, Occasional Paper 21, School for Advanced Urban Studies, University of Bristol.

2. Ibid, p 18.

3. For a detailed account of how AA operates, see Robinson, D. (1979), Talking out of alcoholism: the self-help process of Alcoholics Anonymous, Croom Helm, London.

4. For an interesting discussion of the difficulties of helping problem drinkers in rural areas see Fennell, G. and Wardle, F. (1984), Problem drinking in two matched market towns in Norfolk, School of Economic and Social Studies, University of East Anglia.

5. Tacade/HEC (1984), Alcohol Education Syllabus, Pack 11-16 and Pack 16-19, Tacade, Manchester.

6. Noble, M. (1984), 'The My Body project: its development to date and plans for the future', pp 301-306 in Health Education and Youth edited by Campbell G., Falmer Press, London.

7. A member of the research team sat in on a presentation by the Director of Tacade to a group of Dorset teachers about the Tacade/HEC Alcohol Education Syllabus.

8. Schools Council/HEC (1977), <u>Think well for ages 9-13</u>, Nelson, Walton-on-Thames.

9. The 'round' system of buying drink by young people is discussed by Dorn, N. (1983), <u>Alcohol, youth and the state,</u> Croom Helm, London, pp 178-198. His analysis suggests that the 'round' has different meanings to different strata of young people and that it is very misleading to offer the 'round' as a simple explanation for excessive drinking.

10. Franklin, A. (op cit), p 54.

11. Ibid, p 55.

3

ALCOHOL EDUCATION IN BREATON

The locality

The locality study included the small town of Breaton itself and those surrounding villages and small settlements which naturally gravitate to Breaton to provide for everyday needs. The total population of the area is about 11,600 people. This area is part of a much larger rural district which covers a fifth of the county but houses only a seventh of the population. This rural area is often referred to as not only geographically distinct but also culturally distinct both because of its physical isolation and because of the nature of its economic and social development. In this chapter, reference to 'this rural district' should be taken to mean the larger area rather than Breaton and its surrounding villages, which formed the immediate focus for the locality study.

Iron mining in this rural district, originally developed by the Romans, had lost significance before the turn of the present century. The coal mining which had developed alongside did not decline so rapidly, and in 1951 4,000 people were employed in mining.

The settlement pattern in the area is typified by sporadic developments around the workings of the coal measures. During the 1950s and early 1960s the rapid decline of the coal mining industry revealed the dangers of over-reliance on one source of employment. In 1965, the last coal pit in the district was closed. The coalfield had not given rise to many coal using industries and the main and traditional source of employment was lost.

In the early 1960s the area was characterised by a high average household size and a relatively low number of elderly people and children. There was also a relatively low proportion of professional people and employers, and low car ownership rates. Housing conditions were poor, with over 22% of dwellings lacking the three basic amenities (the national average was 14%).

The decline of coal mining was offset to a small extent by a growth in manufacturing industries - engineering and metals, timber and paper and rubber products. The government was concerned at the lack of employment prospects and offered grants to attract industry. A large company opened a factory in the late 1960s in the northern part of the district, and this provided 4,000 jobs for workers throughout the area, including Breaton, whence busloads of workers were transported daily. In 1982, international competition led to severe cut-backs in employment at the factory and over a period of two or three years the staff was reduced to 1,000 and the Breaton area once again lost its main employer. A local councillor reported that one bus from Breaton now carried around 30 people to the factory.

The county council and district council have begun a programme of developing industrial estates. One of these is in Breaton but nothing like the same level of employment is likely to be achieved as that formerly offered by the industries that have declined.

The Breaton case study area has a large number of drinking outlets relative to the size of the population. There are 46 premises licensed for the sale of alcohol and in addition there are ten registered clubs. This information is summarised in Table 8.

Table 8:   Licensed outlets in the Breaton area

Type of outlet	Number
Public houses, hotels etc with full licence	30
Guest houses and hotels with residents and/or restaurant licence	4
Restaurants	3
Off licences	9
Registered clubs	10
TOTAL	56

31 people were contacted for this locality study. They reflected a range of professional and other interests as shown in Table 9. The rest of the chapter analyses discussions with these 31 people under the same headings as in the previous chapter.

Table 9:   Respondents in the Breaton locality study

Subject area of respondent		Number of respondents
1. Alcohol and specialist provision in the voluntary sector	a) Council on Alcoholism	1
	b) Self help groups	1
2. Alcohol and the NHS	a) Psychiatric services	3
	b) Health education	1
	c) Primary health care	4
3. Counselling services and alcohol education	a) Statutory agencies	9
	b) Voluntary agencies	1
4. Alcohol and the education department	a) Schools	4
	b) The youth service	3
5. Alcohol and the law	a) Police	2
	b) Magistrates	1
6. Miscellaneous	Community Programme project	1

TOTAL   31

Alcohol and specialist provision in the voluntary sector

(a)   The Council on Alcoholism

The Council on Alcoholism covers the whole of the county and began operating in 1964 on a purely voluntary basis. It received no funding, other than a £200 per annum health authority grant, for several years. In 1980 a working party of the joint consultative committee for officers was set up to produce a ten year strategy for the development of services for alcoholics. The working party consisted of representatives of the health authority, social services, the probation service, and the voluntary Council on Alcoholism. Its report recommended that high priority be given to the establishment of a director for the Council. In 1982 a four year joint funding agreement provided £22,000 a year for a director and two part time staff.

The joint funding agreement was between the National Council on Alcoholism and the local health and social services. By 1986 all funding is scheduled to come from within the county, and negotiations over the budgeting for this are causing great concern at the Council. A request for joint finance was being considered by the joint care planning group.

In addition, a grant application was submitted to the South West alcohol education programme for further funding to increase the part time workers' hours and to enable a number of initiatives in educational work to be undertaken.

At the time of the meeting with the director, the Council's office consisted of very limited space made available by the probation service in the second largest town of the county. This lack of suitable accommodation and funding had prevented the Council from embarking upon a training programme for volunteer counsellors. It was hoped that this could be started once the Council had moved to more spacious premises in late 1984, and a funding element for this programme was included in the grant application. (The Council's new premises, situated close to the original office, were occupied in December 1984).

The Council was established in 1964. The present director was appointed in 1982 but had been involved with the Council since 1977. He had lived and worked in the county for many years. The staff consist of a part time counsellor and part time counsellor/secretary. All three have had direct personal experience of alcoholism in themselves or in members of their families, a factor which the director considers useful for a real understanding of the nature of the problem. Membership of the executive committee includes representatives of the social services department, probation, education, NHS, the voluntary sector and the church.

The policy of all Councils on Alcoholism originally aimed at 80% of time on prevention. The local Council had attempted to achieve this but the majority of the staff's working hours were spent in counselling problem drinkers and their families because of the demand for this type of help. All education sessions requested were provided although lack of staff resources meant it was not possible to advertise this service. In the past these pressures meant that administrative work had often been restricted. It had not been possible to pursue plans to open sub-offices in the more rural parts of the county, including the area around Breaton.[1]

In the first nine months of 1984, 774 counselling sessions were held, lasting on average one hour. This involves not only one-to-one interviews but might include family, employer, bank/DHSS officials, and attendance at court hearings. In 1983/84, 78 new problem drinkers were seen, an increase of around 47% over 1982/83. Almost one quarter of these new cases were women, nearly 70% were under 40 years of age, and 48% were unemployed.

Since the appointment of the director in May 1982, 39 people had been referred for in-patient treatment. 15 of them went to the main NHS in-service treatment facilities, two to another NHS hospital and 22 to private sector treatment units. Funding for such placements is often requested from the DHSS.

In addition to counselling, the Council has increasingly become involved in 'home de-tox' treatments in co-operation with the clients' GP. 11 such treatments were given between January 1983 and September 1984, involving Council staff on a daily basis for seven to eight days in each case.

Around 30-40 educational talks are given each year, usually by invitation, to a variety of audiences including schools, youth centres, prison inmates, and local firms. Virtually all educational work is done by the director himself and much of the material used is produced by him, since he feels that most existing material is not good enough. For instance, he frequently uses cartoon drawings in place of photographs. The emphasis is on the effects of abuse. For example, he uses two slides of genuine car accidents and these can shock an audience but, he stresses, the aim is not to preach but to present the facts and let the listener choose. If resources are made available to enable the other staff to take more of the counselling workload, the director would expand educational work. Part of his HEC grant application was for funds for the promotion of sensible drinking to industry, and for training of professionals (especially GPs). Sensible drinking levels are always mentioned and discussed. These levels are based on current HEC thinking and that of the Royal Medical Colleges.

Both the director and the secretary/counsellor had attended a Key Tutor Drinking Choices course and had intended to run their own courses in the county. The director was very critical about the wide degree of choice given to participants which enabled many to 'opt out' of alcohol issues, and concentrate on education and communication aspects. However, he felt that a lot of the course material was very good; courses run in the county would use the manual but restrict choice and emphasise alcohol-specific aspects.

(b)   Self help groups

A representative from Alcoholics Anonymous felt that the number of problem drinkers was around the national level in Breaton but that there was a higher prevalence in the more remote outlying areas around the town. During the eight years that he had been in the area he had observed an increase in the number of women seeking help so that now the meetings were attended mainly by women. He felt that women tended to drink alone at home more than men and sought help earlier. The women were looking for friendship as well as support with their drinking problems whereas men were nearer 'rock bottom' when they asked for help.

He thought that there was quite a lot of under age drinking in the locality. This resulted from a lack of facilities for young people and from pressure on publicans as a result of the economic recession. He felt that there should be tighter restrictions on the sale of alcohol from a whole range of outlets. In addition there should be more education in secondary schools to make young people aware of the problems associated with drinking.

Most people were put in contact with AA by the Samaritans, psychiatrists or hospital social workers: general practitioners were not particularly good at handling problem drinkers. He felt that the word 'alcoholics' was still associated with 'down and outs' in Britain despite the large number of problem drinkers within the professions. He felt that the government failed to acknowledge the extent of the problems caused by drink, in part due to the importance of the revenue generated by alcohol.

Alcohol and the NHS

(a)   Psychiatric services

Prior to 1978 there was no effective NHS alcohol treatment service within the county. This was because the single person employed to help patients with drinking problems took them to alcohol treatment units out of the county.

In 1978 a consultant psychiatrist was appointed with a brief, amongst his other responsibilities, to set up services for patients with drinking problems. He was given a base at a large hospital, which was built in the county town just over a hundred years ago. Initially this consultant's beds were scattered throughout the hospital. In 1980 he was given eight beds on a general psychiatric ward shared with another consultant. The grouping together of the alcohol beds made it possible for nursing staff to begin to specialise in alcohol treatment. In a rationalisation of hospital beds in April 1984, all the consultant's beds were brought together on one ward. This situation, although not ideal, enabled the alcohol beds to be used more flexibly. It also made it possible for the alcohol team to develop a treatment programme.

The team working with the consultant (and dealing with problems in general psychiatry as well as alcoholism) now consists of a psychiatric social worker and a half time psychologist. A community psychiatric nurse specialising in alcoholism has recently been appointed. The patients also have the benefit of other services within the hospital. The art therapy, physiotherapy and occupational therapy departments have made a particular point of putting their specialised resources at the disposal of the patients. Nurses on the ward have steadily built up their expertise, both practically by dealing with the patients, and theoretically by attending appropriate courses. They are founder members of The Association of Nurses in Substance Abuse. Staff are now being recruited for an alcohol day unit, which is expected to open near the town centre in November 1985.

Referrals to the service come principally from general practitioners, although patients are accepted from the hospitals, the courts, the probation service, local social services departments, the local Council on Alcoholism and Alcoholics Anonymous. Local solicitors occasionally ask for assistance with the preparation of clients' defences. Patients are first seen at an out-patient clinic in a nearby town, at home, or at the prison. At that time an assessment is made and a treatment contract agreed.

The contract spells out the aims and objectives of treatment and the part that the patient is expected to play in it. The probation referrals are usually the hardest to deal with because they are often very angry and desolate people.

Treatment consists of a one month stay in hospital during which the patient is detoxified, and then started on a programme which involves individual and group therapy, occupational therapy, and where appropriate, art therapy. As patients are overweight and unfit they are taught the benefits of exercise by the physiotherapy department who also take advantage of the situation to work on group cohesion. The patient is also introduced to outside agencies.

Alcoholics Anonymous meet weekly in the hospital. There is access to Al Anon. The patients' relatives are involved in a relatives' group. Where possible appropriate people from the patient's place of work, occupational health nurses, etc, are brought into the picture.

The use of drugs is kept to the bare minimum. Where patients are cross-addicted to tranquillisers and sleeping pills an attempt is made to reduce, and if possible stop, the intake of those drugs.

When the patient is discharged from the hospital it is anticipated that he or she will attend a local day hospital and proceed from there to out-patient or community follow up. A considerable effort is made to return the patient to the original referring agency in the expectation that the agency will continue to treat the patient using hospital back-up as required.

The consultant said that he often lectured on alcohol issues. These lectures are mainly to other professionals in the health service, the statutory bodies and the voluntary bodies. The aim of the lectures is to raise the awareness of local people to the problems engendered by alcohol, the facilities available to deal with those problems, and the plans for the future. The consultant hopes that increased public awareness will lead to an improvement in funding and resources for the alcohol service.

The consultant sees the Council on Alcoholism as an umbrella organisation bringing together representatives, and thus resources, from all agencies which deal with the problems of alcohol. It has a major responsibility for alcohol education in the county. He appreciates, however, that general education is beyond the Council's resources and feels that the education should be targeted towards 'at risk' groups such as women attending pre-conception clinics, people coming before the courts, publicans, divorcing people, etc. He doubted the value of targeting young people in general, and he cited the example of sex and contraception education as a comparable strategy which he feels has failed. He also wondered if the Council might have a problem in its educational role because it is considered by some as primarily concerned with ex-users.

The consultant said that the improvement in services for those with drinking problems was the result of a great deal of hard work by many people. Overall, he said that debates about the causes and nature of alcoholism tended to be futile and he preferred not to waste time thinking about whether it was an illness or a bad habit with medical aspects.

A consultant psychiatrist works at the Breaton day hospital on one day a week. He is based at the main psychiatric hospital and has special responsibility for the whole of this rural district. The day hospital opened two and a half years ago to serve the adult psychiatric needs of the community. It has facilities for 20 patients per day, providing occupational therapy and various small groups. Some patients attend one or two days per week, a few more often. The day the psychiatrist visits is reserved for the long term patients who "will probably be here forever".

A few of the patients have been referred to the hospital for after-care on discharge from the main psychiatric hospital, but most are referred as outpatients by their GPs. Alcohol is very much a problem for a large proportion of patients though often not directly. He believed only one current patient was 'alcoholic' but for many others alcohol was a complicating factor for themselves or in their family.

He said that heavy drinking in the area was related to the mining days. He felt that it was very difficult to convince local men who regularly drank six pints that such a level might be problematic.

A discussion was also held with an enrolled nurse at the day hospital. Other staff based there included a community psychiatric nurse who was not present. The nurse agreed with the psychiatrist that a significant number of patients were alcohol related cases, but could not say how many. The drink factor might not emerge for some time. For example, a woman presenting with depression might be discovered to have an alcoholic husband.

Group work in the hospital includes a wide range of talks including alcohol related material. Outside the hospital, staff give talks in local schools, mainly about mental health in general. A placement arrangement with the local grammar school enables older pupils to do a period of work in the hospital. In-service training for staff includes talks by the nursing sister in charge of a hostel for alcoholic ex-offenders in the county town.

(b)   Health education

Since reorganisation of the health service in 1982 the Health Education Unit (HEU), based in the main town, has had to cover two district health authorities, one of which includes the area around Breaton. Only two health education officers (HEOs) are in post and one of these explained that the unit was grossly understaffed. A third HEO post is currently vacant, but even when this is filled the unit will still be seven HEOs below the recommended level (one per 50,000 population). This lack of staff resources means that the unit operates as co-ordinator/provider of materials rather than deliverer of education services.

Management of the HEU has recently been shifted from the hospital unit to the community unit and is in a 'state of flux' at present. In addition, a new health promotion group has recently been established, a multi-disciplinary group to advise on priorities. Consequently, the HEU is now more concerned with implementation than with debating the content of programmes.

The overall philosophy of the HEU at present, in view of staffing problems, is to perform fewer tasks but to a higher standard instead of simply responding to external influences and pressures. The priority area for action is heart disease, selected because it has a lot of spin-offs into related areas such as smoking, nutrition and exercise, and also because there was no one else in the area with responsibility for this. The health authority already supports the Council on Alcoholism financially to deal with alcohol education, and does not therefore feel that it should expand its own scarce resources in this field. If approached to do an alcohol education session, the HEO would normally refer the enquirer to the Council.

Although the HEO is a member of the Council on Alcoholism he has little input into its educational work and does not know where the emphasis is put or what message is given. His personal approach would be to use trigger films on how to deal with peer group pressure. Stressing the health damage aspects of alcohol was not effective, particularly amongst working class drinkers whose focus was on short term social and financial costs. Shock tactics have been proved to be very short term in their effect and do not help in the establishment of sensible patterns of consumption. He said that aversion therapy is more effective if one is trying to drive people away from something completely, eg smoking.

The Health Education Unit supports the county council's education department in terms of supplying resources and materials. Health education in schools, until recently, had not been well structured and the only contact was with individual schools asking for materials. The appointment of a social and personal education adviser is seen as an important step in the right direction.

The HEO said that education should be accompanied by pressure on the drinks industry to sell more alcohol-free beers and to market them better. More use should be made of existing laws particularly in relation to drinking drivers. Problems of alcohol abuse are linked directly to fiscal measures and their effect on consumption. Unlike most smokers, the majority of drinkers, even heavy drinkers, are not physically dependent in the sense that they have to maintain a level of alcohol in the blood. Price therefore does have an impact on consumption and even heavy drinkers reduce consumption when the price is high.

(c)   Primary health care

One of the GPs in the only group practice in Breaton was visited. The health visitor attached to this practice was also seen, along with two colleagues based at the Breaton health clinic. One of these was attached to another GP practice and the other was unattached, covering a geographical area around Breaton.

The GP practice was established in 1977 and the GP who was visited joined the practice six years ago. Most of the patients were, therefore, immigrants to the district, although some local people had transferred to the practice. This GP has around 1,500 patients on his list. Of these, he estimates less than 1% have a drink problem. He believes this may be because many of his patients are younger and came into the district because of their appointment to a specific job which gives them a purpose in life. There is a strong relationship between lack of purpose and alcoholism; physical addiction is not the main problem.

Official bodies say GPs are best placed to identify alcohol problems but most would say it is difficult. As a practising homeopath, he keeps detailed 'family profiles' which should enable easier identification of problems. However, GPs can be "a lazy bunch" and they may be reluctant to uncover a drink problem which they had neither the time nor skills to deal with. GPs are not trained at all in alcohol skills and would be more prepared to diagnose a drink problem if there was a community-based alcohol worker - a nurse or social worker - to whom they could refer the patient without taking the major step of referral to acute in-patient treatment. He expressed some concern about whether such referrals received follow up or support if they felt unable to participate in the 'contract' offered by the unit.

The GP prefers to try to handle cases himself by offering counselling but it is very time consuming. Most GPs would be under too much pressure to get involved in counselling patients or in educational work. He tries to educate people at an everyday level in all aspects of health, and feels the media could do more to support health education, to which they give little attention. He has run experimental 'stop smoking' groups in conjunction with the Health Education Unit, but now has no contact with the HEU apart from literature in the post.

The health visitors generally agreed the GPs were not very good at identifying drink problems, particularly since many were themselves prone to alcohol abuse. The role of the health visitor was defined as health education wherever it is needed, but because of time available and community expectations, most effort is directed at child care and very little time is spent on formal health education.

All health visitors are responsible for health education in at least one primary school and the effort put into this obviously varies according to the interest of individual health visitors. There used to be a regular anti-smoking programme but this is only done now if the school requests it. The Health Education Unit has taken over the responsibility for the secondary schools. The top class of the junior school was felt to be the most appropriate age for education in alcohol issues.

Health visitors are free to develop their own particular interests, but all three felt that they needed some alcohol education themselves. They did not know enough either to deal with a problem drinker or to educate people. Ante-natal interviews offer a good opportunity and questions are asked about smoking and drinking; however, they had no alcohol information leaflets to distribute. There was felt to be a gap in their relationship with the Health Education Unit since their previous contact there had left.

The health visitor training course included a session on alcohol from the consultant psychiatrist at the main psychiatric hospital, who also runs occasional in-service training days. There have also been occasional study days on alcohol abuse which have relied heavily on the voluntary agencies.

Counselling services and alcohol education

(a)   Statutory agencies

Six social services personnel were visited: an assistant director whose responsibilities included corporate planning, training and research; two middle managers with special mental health responsibilities; the area director for the whole rural district; and two hospital-based social workers.

The hospital social workers were linked to the consultant psychiatrists at the main psychiatric hospital; both operated very much within the health service world and neither had a great deal of contact with social services area offices. One worked mainly with alcoholic in-patients and followed up selected discharges, usually those with family problems. He saw his role as helping them to see that there were alternative ways to cope with life's problems - relationships, unemployment etc - and to take an initiative to improve matters. He felt field social workers were not very astute at recognising alcohol abuse. He believed that alcohol education would rank quite low as a departmental priority because of the emphasis upon statutory responsibilities.

The assistant director and the area director both questioned the validity of alcohol education, particularly in isolated rural areas where heavy drinking was common and might not be regarded as a problem. Residents would not perceive their drinking as a health issue. The area director had some criticisms of existing treatment and counselling services. He felt that the voluntary sector can seem self-righteous, is resentful of people who can handle drink and does not wish to acknowledge the benefits of alcohol to most people.

Neither saw social services as a reference point for people seeking help with drink problems and neither felt there was a real role for social workers in alcohol education. Generic training would include some basic alcohol education but this was used to refer clients to specialist help. The area director felt that remedial teachers might be the best avenue in schools since they dealt with the educationally non-academic who were most vulnerable to the smoke/drink syndrome.

71

The two middle managers responsible for mental health services explained the lack of professional involvement by social workers in terms of the history of social work training over the past decade and the striving of social workers for recognition of their 'profession'. This has led social workers to interpret their role as dealing only with the problem as presented by the client and not to dig for other underlying factors. Since most clients would present with other problems, eg child care or financial difficulties, the alcohol abuse issue would not be visible. Social workers have not sorted out their professional thinking about alcohol. Many would not like to refer clients to the Council on Alcoholism because this agency would be regarded as anti-alcohol.

The other obstacle to social workers being more willing and able to recognise the alcohol issue was the absence of a proper physical focus for treatment to which clients could be referred. This would be likely to pick up when the new treatment unit opened. Counselling services should be based on this unit not on the Council, whose role should be educational and to act as a pressure group.

Three probation officers were seen, all with responsibilities for the rural district. Two have a particular involvement in alcohol education and the other works mainly in the Breaton locality.

A check on social enquiry reports (SERs) in the rural district over a three month period in 1984 revealed that alcohol was a significant factor in about a third of the cases. This was considered a conservative estimate since it excluded cases for which SERs were not prepared (eg drunken driving) and also those where a possible drink factor was not recognised. Most of the people with whom probation officers came into contact were working class; there would not be much work with middle/upper class offenders except for repeated drink/driving offenders.

The police did not really recognise heavy drinking as a problem unless it led to serious crime, public disorder or offences concerning the use of motor vehicles on roads. Often they did not mention in their report that an offender had been drinking. Some magistrates thought dealing with alcoholism was a matter of will power. They regarded a 'drink factor' as an excuse which they did not like to accept.

Two of the officers had recently started a pilot alcohol education programme (a similar project had been operating in the county town for six years). The aim was to select potential clients and persuade magistrates to make attendance at the programme a condition of probation. The programme consisted of six sessions of group work (one of which was attended by the director of the Council on Alcoholism). At present the tendency was to select the obvious problem drinkers and aim to get them to recognise the part that alcohol was playing in their lives and to motivate them to seek appropriate help from the Council, AA, or hospital.

The officers would like the programme to be more preventive than treatment oriented, working with juveniles who were drinking and at risk of becoming heavy drinkers. However, Home Office directives prevent this since they emphasise work with frequent offenders, not young first offenders, 50% of whom do not re-offend.

It was hoped that the programme would be seen as a resource by other professionals who were presently unwilling to recognise alcohol abuse because there was nowhere to refer clients to. Materials for the programme included two films from the Health Education Unit, but otherwise there was a shortage of good material and a lack of information on what was available. The senior probation officer had attended many conferences and courses on alcohol issues but felt that the programme did not develop because of lack of knowledge. There was also a lack of back-up resources to follow up clients who had been through the programme. Social workers would not want to get involved with a problem drinker unless a child was involved; the Council on Alcoholism may not have the staffing resources to cope with a heavier workload.

Alcohol education should be part of children's general education; teachers probably did not have the time but the Health Education Unit, the police and the Council on Alcoholism could all be used as part of the process. The probation service would like to see a community alcohol team approach - a multi-agency mobilising committee. The people were there but money, materials and co-ordination were lacking.

(b)   Voluntary agencies

The Samaritans are based in the county town and were contacted following a report in a local newspaper that:

73

"local Samaritans have pointed out that the number of
people approaching them over drink problems has risen
by 600% in 10 years."

The director denied the report on the grounds that the Samaritans
did not attempt to classify clients according to type of problem.
She would not agree to be interviewed since they did not have
specific information about nor special skills in dealing with alcohol
issues.   If a client contacted them asking for help with a drink
problem, they would be referred to AA or Al Anon, as appropriate.

Alcohol and the education department

(a)   Schools

The social and personal education adviser (SPEA) had been in post
only nine months at the time of the meeting with the research
team.   There had been a gap between his predecessor's departure
and his appointment and he had spent much of his time simply
getting himself known in the schools.   His role in social and
personal education is only 50% of his job (he is also general adviser
to 24 schools in a defined geographical area); therefore, he has
tended to operate in a reactive rather than proactive way so far.
He defined his role as providing advice on methods, materials and
media, and providing in-service training for teachers.

He feels that the educationalist's model of alcohol education may
be different from that adopted by the Council on Alcoholism.   The
school's focus may be upon sensible and socially acceptable
drinking behaviour; the Council's primary focus may be upon the
rehabilitation of problem drinkers and their families.   Education
should be developmental not geared to the treatment of a problem.
He believes there is no logic in a model which sees alcohol as
addictive for everyone; some people may have a genetic
predisposition to becoming addicted, but there are very many other
variables which act in unknown combinations, and those who are
susceptible to these pressures are more likely to become addicted.

The educationalist's role is built on the premise that alcohol is
socially acceptable (although it would probably be banned as a
dangerous drug if invented today), that it has positive social
benefits and that although people will go through periods of
experimentation, most will not become addicted.   Negative aspects
such as drinking and driving also should be stressed.

In the past, health education has often been limited to giving information. He feels that it is simplistic to think that just giving information leads to changes in attitudes or behaviour. There are three factors which intervene between knowing and doing:

(i)   The 'internal me' - values and beliefs

(ii)   Behaviour of influential others

(iii)   Social context

Any materials for alcohol education need to get people to look at these issues as well as information about alcohol and its effects.

The adviser is at present writing a chapter concerning current tensions and trends in school health education which comments upon the effectiveness of a range of teaching approaches, eg the shock-horror approach, information giving, resisting social pressures. He believes that school alcohol programmes should place particular emphasis on how young people may resist social pressures associated with the offer of alcoholic drinks in a range of social settings. This requires more participative forms of teaching and many teachers would have to change their teaching style because of their heavy reliance on straight information giving. Schools, through their involvement in external examinations, may place high priority on the achievement of short-term measurable outcomes. Health education, does not lend itself to such assessment of effectiveness. In some schools, health education courses are staffed by teachers who have surplus time available after their academic teaching commitment has been met. Even in schools where they try to select staff with a commitment, they are still unable to give it the same priority as mathematics, science etc.

Discussions were held with three teachers involved in social education at the two secondary schools in Breaton. Two of these three were from the secondary modern school, serving mainly the area around Breaton, and one was from the grammar school whose catchment area was the whole of the rural district. In September 1985 a comprehensive education system is being introduced into the area; the two present schools will combine up to fifth year and a separate tertiary college will be established.

In the secondary modern school, social education starts in the first year with all years receiving one period per week. Four teachers are responsible for these lessons; for fourth and fifth years, the same period is timetabled and managed by these four to permit maximum flexibility. A common teaching method used is to have the pupils operate in small groups, interviewing a visitor (lower years often choose their own visitors). Up to 15 different people might be invited on any one occasion and each group prepares its own questions and manages the session. The whole ethos of the social education programme is to teach pupils to take responsibility for their own lives and their own decisions, not to preach to them. Health education is mainly covered in the fourth year and there is also an element in the fifth year course about relationships.

Alcohol education could come into both these elements. Previous visitors to the fourth and fifth year include members of AA and Al Anon. The pupils really respond to the 'personal tale' approach. In connection with alcohol education, use is also made of The Jimmy Greaves Story on video which is very useful since he is a personality the children can relate to.

Tutorial groups in the third and fourth year also have an element of alcohol education in the programme - mainly providing factual information about alcohol.

Social education in the grammar school is by means of a Design for Living programme which was begun around 1972. This programme is for fifth and sixth form pupils only. Around three years ago an attempt was made to extend it down to third and fourth years, but this was strongly resisted by staff who were opposed to giving up time from other subjects. Fourth years do now have one period a week, but this is mainly careers education. Nothing is done in the area of social education for the first three years.

The respondent at this school said that in the early years, staff involved in the programme were very committed and produced a lot of their own material; as they left, staff who were not quite so enthusiastic took over. The present team consists of six teachers and the course was perhaps more narrow in outlook. Apart from the biological facts of reproduction in the first year, there is no sex education till fifth form. A health education officer is then brought in to do a session on sex and venereal disease, but this has to be just information-giving with no discussion on relationships, morals etc.

The Design for Living programme includes two long courses on censorship and crime, and four sessions on various health issues from a health education officer. Virtually all health education is done by visiting speakers. There is no specific alcohol education content to the programme, although it may well come up under various other topics. After reorganisation in September, social education in the new comprehensive school will be the responsibility of the fifth year tutor who currently teaches at the grammar school. He intends to establish social education as a logical progression from first year upwards (rather like the secondary modern school at present).

All three of the teachers were asked whether drinking amongst pupils was a cause for concern amongst staff. The teacher at the grammar school said he drank only very occasionally himself, and thought that alcohol was not regarded as a particularly important issue by staff or pupils. He knew that some pupils did use pubs and clubs, that there was nowhere else to go, but "they seem to be sensible drinkers". Besides, academic youngsters do not have as much money to spend on drink as those on the dole or YTS schemes.

The two teachers at the secondary modern school were concerned about pupils' drinking and related a few incidents where they had had to take home pupils of 15 and 16 who had been "on a binge". They felt that there was a lot of under age drinking going on in pubs and especially in clubs, very often with the knowledge and approval of parents.

(b)   The youth service

The youth and community services officer responsible for the whole of the rural district and the youth leader and warden of Breaton youth centre were both contacted. Also visited was a local politician who was, inter alia, chairman of the Breaton youth club and president of the football club.

The youth and community services officer explained that whilst he and other senior managers were based in the education department, the rest of the service staff, including youth leaders, were part of the recreation and leisure department. There are six full time youth and community wardens in the rural district; five of these are club-based, and one works throughout the area supporting local management committees and the 40 to 60 part time youth workers who run activities in many of the small villages. In the Breaton area, in addition to the purpose-built youth club, there are clubs in several of the villages, while the rugby club has a strong policy of organising youth teams and social events.

This officer said that youth leaders are very much building-based and since drink is not allowed into the clubs, they may not feel affected by the alcohol issue. They would only take an initiative if alcohol was seen to be affecting their centre. He would like to see youth workers operating out from their bases more, but this would require a policy change. This is not easy to effect with today's extreme financial problems. It would also mean workers having to change their whole approach to their jobs, and then they would recognise the alcohol issue. At present, if a leader knows someone has been drinking before coming to the club he would admit him/her unless obviously the worse for wear. This often happens on disco nights when youngsters go to the public house first and bring cans and bottles with them to consume outside.

He felt under age drinking is done openly in many public houses and clubs by 16 year olds who do not really consider themselves to be breaking the law. Some pubs and sports clubs exist totally on young people's custom; they have the money to spend, even if they are on the dole, more so if on a YTS scheme and living at home. Under 16s tend to buy alcohol at supermarkets and off licences.

The youth officer said that alcohol is more of an issue in this area than the abuse of solvents and illegal drugs. Drink is regarded by young people as a socially acceptable way of getting high, whereas drugs are known to be unacceptable. The officer was very concerned about the use of alcohol by young people because of the problems it creates in youth centres and schools, because it leads to bad behaviour and vandalism within the community, and because young people are abusing themselves and are being abused by local retailers and publicans who know that they are supplying under age people.

The youth leader at Breaton agreed that youngsters of 14 and 16 years who use the club do drink off the premises, mostly getting it from supermarkets where they can be served by 18 or 19 year olds who knew them at school. Occasionally, someone comes in drunk and the leader telephones the parents. However, the young people who use the club are ones from 'better' families; those most likely to drink a lot would tend to be those who would not attend youth clubs.

The rise in unemployment over the past three years in Breaton has created a dramatic change in families' standards of living; parents under stress are not supporting their youngsters and turn their backs on the fact that 14 year olds are drinking.

The youth leader initiates informal discussions with young people in the club as the need arises over a variety of issues. He feels particularly strongly about dissuading them from smoking. Sometimes role play exercises are done and tape-recorded. Youth clubs have to be careful to ensure that these sort of things are done in an entertaining way; youngsters do not go to clubs to be given more lessons.

Both these staff were aware of educational material available from the Health Education Unit but felt that they needed better material, more interesting films and a less passive approach by the HEU. More literature should be sent to youth leaders pushing them to take up available resources rather than just responding to requests. Youth leaders have very little time to attend courses and do not have enough information about what is available.

The chairman of the youth club was also concerned at the problem of under age drinking since he saw this as leading directly to vandalism. An attempt had been made at the youth club to establish an 18+ club for ex-members; a bar was set up and the steward was told not to sell to people who had had too much. The aim was to show sensible drinking habits to younger people, but the club failed because the bar did not sell enough.

All three respondents were very critical of the way existing laws were not being enforced to curb the sale of drink to under age people.

Alcohol and the law

(a)   The police

The chief inspector responsible for the county-wide community services department explained that his department was responsible for crime prevention, road safety, juvenile liaison and press and public liaison, including schools. The chief inspector described his job as involving the co-ordination of police community activities and this inevitably involved attending a considerable number of meetings. The police regard alcohol as a cause for concern in so far as it affects their ability to achieve certain objectives, for example, the prevention of nuisance and the preservation of peace and tranquillity. Events such as discos which attract a lot of people might lead to gang fights. Police reports to the licensing meetings indicate an increase in 1984 in public order offences, many of which are drink related. Motoring offences involving

79

alcohol are also on the increase.

75% of petty criminals caught had been drinking. Real professionals do not drink before doing a job and do not get caught. Most juvenile offences are committed by 15-16 year olds; then they start to grow out of it. For most youngsters it is the same with alcohol; it is part of the growing up process and they learn to cope better with peer group pressure as they get older. More police are now recognising alcoholism as an illness, and forces are adopting policies of cautioning rather than prosecuting drunkenness cases. His police authority had not yet explored this possibility because of the pressure of other commitments.

The department's educational work involves talks to community groups, youth clubs etc. It has also been involved in a drink-driving campaign aimed at juvenile drinkers. Work in schools is based on a 'Schools involvement programme', a series of talks on various topics which is circulated to all heads who then request particular elements. Focused approaches may be made to particular schools where a specific problem is perceived.

The programme includes a talk entitled 'The law and you', aimed at the 14+ age groups. The talk covers five areas: alcohol, drugs, solvent abuse, motor cycles and cars, and offensive weapons. The alcohol element lists alcohol related offences and touches on social consequences and physical effects of drinking. The message is that it is not necessary not to drink, but that it is necessary to drink responsibly. Whilst alcohol is dealt with first, the sections on drugs and solvent abuse are longer and more detailed.

The inspector at Breaton stated that drink related offences are not a particularly serious problem in the area although he believes that drinking problems are on the increase. It is not always possible for the police to show or ascertain that an offence is drink related. There was an obvious correlation between public order offences and time of day, eg the peak time for assaults is 11.00 pm. Other offences where alcohol is likely to be involved, eg marital assaults, would not usually lead to charges.

Table 10: Convictions for selected offences in the Breaton police area

	1983	1984
(a) Alcohol related offences		
Licensee breaching licensing law	-	1
Juvenile buying intoxicating liquor	-	1
Drunkenness	2	2
Driving/in charge of vehicle, with excess alcohol	23	17
(b) Public order offences		
Assault	21	25
Criminal damage	51	54
Disorderly behaviour	4	7

The low level of prosecutions for under age drinking partly reflects the difficulties in enforcing the law. It is not easy for a licensee to tell if a person is under 18 years and police do not have the resources to check each possibility individually. This inspector also believes that 'young lads' drink in clubs rather than pubs; police control is less easy to enforce in registered clubs and really relies on persuading management committees to heed advice. He felt there was no evidence of drinking on the streets and concluded that not much alcohol was being purchased by young people at off licences and supermarkets.

The Breaton police report for 1984 to the annual licensing meeting states that:

> "Advice has been given on certain occasions to licensees where it was known or suspected that the licensing laws were not being strictly complied with."

This reflects the general attitude of the police in Breaton to licensed premises staying open after hours. A first offender would not be prosecuted but would be given a warning. All licensed premises are visited regularly by the police and the police always act when complaints are made about noise.

Since alcohol misuse is not seen as a priority problem it has not been a subject for educational sessions. The police do have an officer at Breaton who co-ordinates a programme of school visits, and talks are also given to other community groups, usually on subjects which the group requests. The inspector is unsure of the potential role of the police in alcohol education and feels that police do not have sufficient information and knowledge about alcohol issues.

(b)   Magistrates

The Magistrate interviewed emphasised that she was giving her own personal views. Breaton is not considered to be a heavy drinking area, but for young people social life centres around pubs and also clubs (where children are taken). She is convinced that many of the young men prosecuted for petty offences have been drinking although they do not get recorded as alcohol related offences, and it does not appear in any statistics. When probation reports are requested, alcohol is very often mentioned.

She sees the social acceptability of drink as the main factor for not tackling the alcohol/crime relationship. She considers a high percentage of all cases have a drink factor.

Despite having been a vociferous anti-smoking campaigner she is pessimistic about alcohol education because of the strong drink lobby in Parliament, and the influence of television. She can see benefits in the elderly and terminally ill drinking moderately. She has managed to 'indoctrinate' her own children against alcohol.

Miscellaneous

The Community Programme project

The manager of the local Community Programme project explained that this project is funded by the Manpower Services Commission (MSC) and managed by a committee of the Diocese which is the sponsoring body. At present 21 people are in post. Funds will be available for up to 37, mostly aged between 18 and 25, including five young women. Workers carry out jobs for people in the community, particularly elderly or disabled people, including gardening, decorating, and minor repair jobs. The premises, an old school building, house engineering and carpentry workshops and provide accommodation for a local pre-school playgroup. A canteen/recreation room for the workers is also provided. Around 50% of work time is spent renovating and maintaining the premises.

The project had a lot of management problems in the past and these had led to bad publicity locally. These problems have not been totally resolved and it appears that the management is still preoccupied with these issues.

Young people who are referred to the project by the Job Centre tend to be those who have been unable to find work elsewhere. Most of the young men are considered to be low achievers and several are said to have behavioural problems. The manager does not think that the workers drink heavily and there is not much talk about drinking. He is the only person interviewed who considers that drug abuse is probably more of a problem than alcohol abuse, though he has no real evidence of either.

Lack of money is considered to be a reason for not drinking; workers are paid £46.80 for three days' work a week. The manager is concerned that if young people are found permanent jobs by the project, as sometimes happens, they might find themselves with £200 a week and could afford to go out every night. Alcohol education is needed to stop them spending it all on booze.

The project premises are also used by a local intermediate treatment group. The manager believes that most of the boys would be at risk at home from violent fathers who drink heavily. He feels there is some scope for alcohol education on the project but is unsure what this might involve.

Alcohol education in Breaton and the South West programme

As in the Cornford study, respondents were asked whether they had heard about the South West alcohol education programme. Only seven of the 30 respondents had been aware of the programme prior to the research team's contact; and of these seven, three appeared to know little more than the fact that a programme was proposed. None of the seven were professional workers based within the Breaton locality; all of them had county or sub-county level responsibilities and most were involved in specialist treatment or educational services. Table 11 summarises the responses. Since the programme would not be launched publicly in the area until November 1985, it is not surprising that so few fieldworkers were aware of it. Most of those who did know had either personally been invited or belonged to agencies which had been invited to the initial exploratory meetings in 1984.

There was support amongst these seven respondents for the general aims of the programme but reservations, sometimes conflicting, were expressed about the emphasis in its methods and organisation. One respondent involved in treatment and counselling felt that too much emphasis was placed on communication/educational aspects and not enough on stressing the dangers of alcohol abuse. On the other hand an educationalist, seen in May 1985, expressed concern over the future management of the programme, fearing that it might become too crisis-orientated rather than educational.

Two respondents expressed dissatisfaction with the availability of information about the programme. One found it "difficult to keep track of what's happening". The other complained that he had put his name down for the Drinking Choices course, but received no papers and later found that he had missed it.

Overall, the alcohol education structure in the Breaton area reflects the locality's isolation from the central management of services in the two main towns of the county. On a county level, the Council on Alcoholism is regarded as the focus of the alcohol education network; its membership includes senior management of the social services and probation service, the health service treatment and educational personnel, the police and representatives of the voluntary sector and the church. The statutory services have been willing for the Council itself to take on the main responsibility for alcohol education and therefore accord it low priority within their own organisations.

Within the Breaton area, a number of agencies do, on a local basis, get involved in various aspects of social and health education. These initiatives have tended to focus on young people, often organised by the schools as part of social education programmes. Participation in these events was mentioned and considered valuable by many respondents, including the GP, health visitors, youth leaders, probation officers, police and psychiatric nurse. Several of these professionals were enthusiastic about a more specific alcohol education content within these programmes, but clearly felt a lack of support in terms of guidance and materials.

At this local level the Council on Alcoholism had had little impact and was certainly not seen as the agency to turn to for such support. The gap was clearly felt to be between the Health Education Unit and grass-root workers. Some respondents were concerned about not knowing whom to relate to in the Unit, and not making information and materials more accessible.

Table 11: Knowledge of the South West alcohol education programme

Subject area of respondent		Number of respondents	Aware of programme	Unaware of programme
1. Alcohol and specialist provison in the voluntary sector	a) Council on Alcoholism	1	1	0
	b) Self help groups	1	0	1
2. Alcohol and the NHS	a) Psychiatric services	3	1	2
	b) Health education	1	1	0
	c) Primary health care	4	0	4
3. Counselling services and alcohol education	a) Statutory agencies	9	2	7
	b) Voluntary agencies	1	0	1
4. Alcohol and the education department	a) Schools	4	1	3
	b) The youth service	3	0	3
5. Alcohol and the law	a) Police	2	1	1
	b) Magistrates	1	0	1
6. Miscellaneous	Community Programme project	1	0	1
TOTALS		31	7	24

Fieldworkers were willing to get involved, but felt they needed positive encouragement to do so.

Drinking patterns and problems in Breaton

As in the previous chapter, it is very difficult to draw firm conclusions about drinking patterns in the Breaton area. The chapter is far more illuminating about professionals than it is about local residents, a fact which will be considered in more detail in the final chapter.

At this stage, a few general points can be made. There was a clear tendency amongst professionals, mainly those who were based outside the villages, to stress that heavy drinking was part of 'the cultural tradition' and that it would be hard to challenge or change. A number of the 31 respondents perceived local people to be somehow different from themselves, drinking being a more central element in their lifestyle.

As with the other three case studies, respondents were keen to discuss youthful drinking. This was seen as widespread and to be mainly carried out in pubs and social clubs where very little concern was expressed about under age drinking or the strict adherence to the laws about opening hours. Respondents saw this as reprehensible although very difficult to challenge. Considerable concern was expressed about unemployment. This was seen as undermining the morale of some parents who did not make major efforts to control the behaviour of children, especially in areas such as teenage drinking. Young people were seen as depressed about their future job prospects and therefore tempted by self destructive lifestyles. Only one respondent saw this behaviour as including illegal drugs and solvents as well as alcohol.

References

1.   As indicated in Chapter Two, the difficulties of developing services for problem drinkers in rural areas is discussed in Fennell, G. and Wardle, F. (1984), Problem drinking in two matched market towns in Norfolk, School of Economic and Social Studies, University of East Anglia.

4
ALCOHOL EDUCATION IN WESTCROSS AND LYNCOMBE

The locality

Westcross has a population of approximately 19,000 and is the administrative centre for the borough council and the headquarters of a large multi-national company which dominates the local labour market. Lyncombe is a small coastal village of 2,000 residents and it is five miles from Westcross. When the smaller settlements between Westcross and Lyncombe are added, the locality study area covers just over 22,000 people according to the 1981 census.

Westcross developed as a market town in the 12th and 13th centuries. Employment in the town has been dominated since the 18th century by various forms of mining or extractive industry. There have been large variations in the market for these commodities at different times and, as a result, the mining industry has experienced numerous booms and collapses. In the late 19th century, many miners emigrated from Westcross to America, Australia and South Africa as a result of one such collapse.

The instability of the local mining industry in this period was heightened by the number of very small producers. One of the main extracted commodities was a substance used in pottery and paper making. The 19th and early 20th century saw a complex process of amalgamations and takeovers within this particular mining industry. The end result has been the development of the large multi-national company referred to above. This company is now concerned with much more than just mining. It has over 12,000 employees in five separate divisions that include mining, transport, leisure and construction interests. Not all of these employees work in Westcross, indeed an increasing number work abroad. However, the local development plan of the borough council stated that in 1976 this company employed 6,500 people or one third of the workforce in the employment exchange area. Mining jobs had declined through mechanisation (2,000 jobs lost between 1961 and 1971) but this had been balanced by the diversification of the company into leisure, joinery and tourism. This plan also stated that the mining industry employed 2,300 people in pits and 2,800 people in ancillary tasks (engineering, transport and office work), although not all of them were the direct employees of the main company. This situation has remained broadly the same in subsequent years. There have been no large scale redundancies and unemployment remains relatively low. Westcross has been spared the worst effects of the recession.

In the first quarter of the 20th century, Westcross remained a market town of around 4,000 people. The real expansion of the town began from the 1960s onwards. Not only was the mining industry continuing to expand but the area was also eligible for government regional assistance and this encouraged a considerable increase in house building, especially to the East of the town centre. As a result, the town centre remains on the Western fringe of the overall settlement. As the town spread backwards, smaller villages were assimilated into Westcross. These places already had their own churches, shops and pubs, and residents still relate to their old village centres. Nearly all of this house building was for owner occupation and there is little post war council housing in Westcross. Council houses were concentrated in a nearby parish which is four miles from Westcross and outside the case study area.

The county is often noted as both an important tourist centre and as a retirement area. Westcross does not fit neatly into this picture. It is a market town with a strong manufacturing base and service sector; tourists pass through Westcross or use its shops, cinema and other facilities on a rainy day but it is not a tourist centre. The small coastal village of Lyncombe, however, is much closer to the stereotypical view of county settlements. It is a picturesque fishing village that attracts both tourists and retirers.

There are several 'popular' histories of Lyncombe that are geared to the tourist market and most of these focus on the accounts of older residents of life in the village between the wars, when employment was dominated by fishing, especially for pilchards. Lyncombe comes over as an enclosed community, hostile to the outside world. It remains a busy fishing harbour, although this industry has experienced numerous 'ups and downs'. Fishing declined after the second world war but picked up in the late 1960s through mackerel fishing. Over-fishing after entry to the EEC created further problems but there are now stricter regulations to protect fish stocks. About 30 boats work from the harbour although many of them concentrate upon tourist fishing trips in the summer months. Tourism is now a central industry in Lyncombe, which is both a tourist base and, perhaps more importantly, a major attraction for day visitors because of the attractive harbour and surrounding buildings.

The Westcross and Lyncombe case study area has a large number of drinking outlets relative to the size of the population although this statement is obviously complicated by the size of the tourist influx in the summer into the case study area. There are 114 premises licensed for the sale of alcohol and, in addition, there are 19 registered clubs. This information is summarised in Table 12.

Table 12:   Licensed outlets in Westcross and Lyncombe

Type of outlet	Number
Public houses, hotels etc with full licence	24
Guest houses, hotels, holiday parks etc with resident, resident/restaurant or restricted licence	46
Restaurants	18
Off licences	26
Registered clubs	19
TOTAL	133

In Westcross, town centre public houses and hotels are largely dependent upon the lunchtime trade and most place a heavy emphasis upon the sale of food. Westcross town centre is largely deserted in the evenings; residents tend to use licensed outlets in their village centre rather than travel to the town centre. In Lyncombe, there is a much more marked contrast between the winter and summer trade. The five outlets with full licences, the seven licensed restaurants and two off licences largely depend on the summer trade. This is even more true of the 17 outlets which have either a residential, residential/restaurant or restricted licence.

In Westcross and Lyncombe, 47 respondents were contacted, although three of them were by telephone only. Table 13 lists the categories into which these can be broken down.

Table 13: Discussions held for the Westcross and Lyncombe locality study

Subject area of respondent		Number of respondents
1. Alcohol and specialist provision in the voluntary sector	a) Council on Alcoholism	5
	b) Self help groups	1
2. Alcohol and the NHS	a) The psychiatric service	2
	b) Health education	1
	c) Schools of nursing	1
	d) Primary health care	5
3. Counselling services and alcohol education	a) Statutory agencies	5
	b) Voluntary agencies	3
	c) The churches	2
4. Alcohol and the education department	a) Schools	7
	b) The youth service	3
	c) Colleges of Further Education	5
5. Alcohol and the law	a) Police	2
	b) Magistrates	1
6. Miscellaneous		4
TOTAL		47

Alcohol and specialist provision in the voluntary service

(a)   The Council on Alcoholism

The Council on Alcoholism for the county is based in Westcross. The Council evolved out of the former South West Council on Alcoholism which was formed in 1966. The South West Council initially covered four counties and was based 100 miles away. However, a retired miner, who was a member of AA, offered his house in Westcross as a regular stopping point for the director of the South West Council. The director built up his contact with locally based agencies, especially the probation service. The resultant grants combined with fund raising produced £5,000 and this qualified for a £5,000 grant from the DHSS. A new Council on Alcoholism was thus established.

In the early years of its existence, this Council was primarily a route into AA. The present director did not become involved until 1975. For much of the 1970s and early 1980s there was a fight for survival because of lack of funds, a situation not helped by conflict with the National Council on Alcoholism. The financial situation has eased since 1983 when re-affiliation with the National Council opened the way for a pump priming grant from DHSS. Joint finance funding of £30,000 per annum for three years was obtained. A further large grant was obtained from the Manpower Services Commission (MSC) to employ workers to initiate a range of activities.

The Council employs five main 'professional' staff, three of whom are members of the British Association for Counselling. The director not only takes major responsibility for policy development but remains actively engaged in numerous counselling activities. There is a full time senior counsellor who is a trained group worker, a part time education officer who is an ex-school teacher and a part time secretary/administrator. The MSC money is used to fund a former psychiatric nurse who has been involved in a range of counselling and research activities. The director of the Council on Alcoholism is responsible to an Executive Committee of 24 members. The members of this Committee are, on the whole, of high status and considerable influence in both the public and private sector in the county. This is seen as enabling the Council on Alcoholism to work easily with a wide range of agencies.

The director and his staff felt it was possible to define five main areas of work, namely counselling, training, information giving, education and administration. With regard to counselling, clients or their families usually phone in on the 9 to 5 service although there was also a regular supply of referrals from other agencies. In 1984, 1,432 interviews were carried out with clients and their relatives of which 670 were with men and 762 were with women. The senior counsellor believed that a flexible model should be used for counselling. The clients should be encouraged to determine their own problems, options and goals. Their only rule was that they would not see people who have had alcohol on the day. However, the staff found it helpful to conceptualise their work and its relationship to the problems of clients in the way outlined in

Table 14.   Detoxification is carried out by medical staff.   This scheme emphasised that the primary issue to be addressed was the 'original problems' of the client, but that these could not be tackled until heavy drinking had been overcome.   The director stressed that there was a place for the sensible use of alcohol in society; abstinence was not necessarily a goal for problem drinkers and being dry did not necessarily mean being recovered and happy.

In recent years, there had been an expansion of work in the areas of training, education and information supply.   Council staff were attempting to make such work part of integrated courses or training schedules rather than being sucked into an endless stream of one-off talks.   The full extent of this work was illustrated by the paper presented to one of the early briefing conferences for the South West alcohol education programme.   The following list was provided:

(a)   25 visits were made to schools and colleges in the county to give talks or to participate in group sessions.

(b)   Staff from the Council on Alcoholism participated in three events organised by the health education department and were also involved in HEC Look after yourself tutor training events.

(c)   Six visits were made to youth training schemes.

(d)   Numerous student nurses and trainee social workers visited the Council or were placed with it.

(e)   A further seven training events received an input from Council staff.

(f)   Five main training courses were run by the Council.   For example, an alcohol education programme of eight weekly sessions was run for people in trouble with the law through drink.   The main aim was to educate participants about the damage alcohol could cause.   The programme was run jointly by the Council on Alcoholism and the probation service.

(g)   There was a range of training, development and research activities sponsored under the MSC Community Programme (eg research into the accommodation needs of problem drinkers).

Table 14: Counselling and the 'problem' drinker

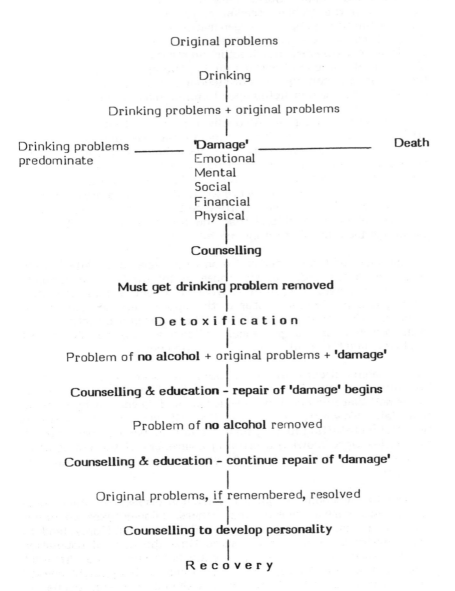

Original problems
|
Drinking
|
Drinking problems + original problems
|

Drinking problems ———— **'Damage'** ———————— Death
predominate   Emotional
                            Mental
                            Social
                            Financial
                            Physical
|
Counselling
|
Must get drinking problem removed
|
D e t o x i f i c a t i o n
|
Problem of **no alcohol** + original problems + **'damage'**
|
Counselling & education – repair of 'damage' begins
|
Problem of **no alcohol** removed
|
Counselling & education – continue repair of 'damage'
|
Original problems, <u>if</u> remembered, resolved
|
Counselling to develop personality
|
R e c o v e r y

What the above list failed to clarify was the overall balance of this education and training work. How much was designed to address the needs of the problem drinker or to explain the availability of services for this group to the general population? How much was designed to address issues of sensible drinking in the general population? However, the director did stress that it was wrong to discuss drink in general without taking the opportunity to warn of the dangers and consequences of alcohol abuse. A failure to do this trivialised the harm inflicted upon families from problem drinking.

Staff at the Council on Alcoholism stressed that it was very difficult to obtain a 'feel' for drinking patterns and 'problems' in the Westcross locality. They suspected that many young people, especially those in villages, had nowhere to meet but the public house. They suspected under age drinking was widespread from twelve years onwards. They were worried that home brewing was a sizeable problem. In general, they felt local people were badly informed about alcohol and that the presence of tourists might encourage local people to drink more.

Six members of the Executive Committee were also visited. Four of these discussions, namely those with the GP, community psychiatric nurse, consultant psychiatrist and senior probation officer, will be discussed later in the appropriate section of this chapter. The other two were with the managing director of the local brewery and a personnel officer at the town's largest employer, and these will be briefly outlined now.

The managing director of the brewery had been on the Executive Committee of the Council on Alcoholism for 15 years and he confirmed there had been numerous 'ups and downs', many of them financial. However, he felt the Council was on a much firmer financial and staffing footing than it had ever been before. Health authorities were showing a growing awareness of the problems of alcohol abuse and Councils on Alcoholism were no longer seen as 'crackpot'.

He saw the alcoholic as suffering from a disease to which some people were more susceptible than others. Higher taxes would not stop an alcoholic while reduced availability would only lead to more 'meths' drinking. At the same time the general population required education about drink. The alcoholic strength of different drinks had to be understood; the importance of bodyweight needed appreciation. Both teachers and GPs should be better trained in this area. GPs often failed to diagnose alcohol related illness.

Teachers did not warn children of the dangers of alcohol or they addressed this issue in a way that created a mystique. Getting the balance of the message right was difficult; drink did reduce anxiety and had many positive benefits for most people. The positive aspects of drink could be maximised if people drank in the public houses rather than the home. However, pubs needed to provide a pleasant drinking environment; they should be regarded as a place to relax and meet friends and not to blot out all the cares of the world.

The 'pub scene' was changing.[1] Beer sales peaked in the late 1970s. Lager now represented 40% of beer sales while wine consumption was also growing. Public houses were now trying to attract women and children; family rooms were being opened and food sales were a significant source of income for most landlords.[2] Village pubs owned by his brewery were encouraged to provide a service for the whole community and not just the young. However, other pubs did gear themselves to the youth market. Monitoring under age drinking was almost impossible. A surfeit of licences had developed in the county because of the tourist trade; sales in winter were low and landlords were often desperate for a sale. The Licensed Victuallers were trying to persuade local magistrates to block new licence applications.

The personnel officer stressed that alcoholism was a disease that required treatment. It stemmed from a complex mix of susceptibility because of genetically defined metabolism, emotional instability and mental problems. Alcohol was a crutch for the inadequate. Information about alcoholics needed to be fed into a data bank from which software packages could be developed on treatment for the alcoholic and support for the spouse and children. Effective treatment involved three main components. First, good facilities were required for drying out. Second, counselling based on transactional analysis[3] needed to be available so that the deep origins of emotional instability could be tackled. Third, physical fitness was essential because it enabled people to cope with the stresses of everyday life. He was sceptical about the value of alcohol education. If one was fit, heavy drinking was no problem. His father was a miner and drank heavily most days; he was 85 and fine. However, he did not feel alcohol was a big issue for the future compared to unemployment. People in the county believed in the work ethic because of the strength of Methodism. In the future, there would be less and less permanent work. This would cause enormous stress within individuals.

Most of those involved with the Council on Alcoholism stressed to the research team that one key problem was the rural nature of the county. The catchment area around Westcross now had an effective service. However, the staff and resources were not yet available to provide an equivalent service for every other market town and village in the county.

(b)   Self help groups

One member of an Alcoholics Anonymous group in Westcross was visited. He suggested that there was considerable tension between local AA groups and both the Council on Alcoholism and the psychiatric hospital. Senior staff at the hospital are seen as hostile to the philosophy of AA. They directed patients to the Council on Alcoholism which pretended there was an easy way out. AA group meetings started from a recognition that each member was an alcoholic and needed group support and massive will power to stay abstinent. The role of education was to inform people where they could obtain help if they suffered from the disease of alcoholism. Some people were destined to be alcoholics. Education could not stop this inevitable process.

Alcohol and the NHS

(a)   The psychiatric service

A consultant psychiatrist from the main psychiatric hospital in the district health authority was seen. She was a member of the Executive Committee of the Council on Alcoholism and very committed to service development for problem drinkers.

However, her post as consultant psychiatrist made no special reference to alcohol and there was initially no alcohol recovery service within the health authority. If people became physically ill with alcohol, they were taken into hospital until they were well enough to leave and resume their drinking. However, this consultant had been able to instigate the beginnings of a recovery service for alcoholics despite opposition. Drying out was now offered at her hospital together with individual and group therapy sessions where the director of the Council on Alcoholism played a crucial role. A community psychiatric nurse had been persuaded to become involved in this work while ex-patients were encouraged to become active members of the Council on Alcoholism. AA also held meetings at the hospital although the consultant expressed some anxiety that their approach could become too narrow at times. AA offered only one solution. The patient might find this solution inappropriate and the whole experience of AA involvement could then prove psychologically damaging.

The consultant believed that the geography of the county meant that there was a need for local groups to carry out counselling and group therapy. The ideal pattern would be resources in the community combined with a central hospital unit. Community resources might include the ability to carry out home detoxifications. The central unit could provide in-patient care, which some people needed, since it provided treatment in a closed environment; this unit could also be a centre for expertise, information and training. Such a model still retained an important role for the Council on Alcoholism, which offered a 'walk in' counselling service; it was heavily involved in the essential areas of prevention and training. However, the health authority was in general unsympathetic towards allocating more resources for alcohol treatment or education. Financial support for the Council on Alcoholism was sometimes used to justify this negative attitude.

This consultant perceived problem drinking as a complex disease process with multiple causes. There was a wide range of consequences for the sufferer who was affected physically, emotionally, socially and economically. A complex disease required complex treatment and all the consequences had to be tackled by those with the relevant skills. A simple medical model was not appropriate and so doctors found it difficult to address the needs of problem drinkers. The medical profession needed to learn how to work with a wide range of public and voluntary agencies in helping such people.

Alcohol abuse was a massive problem in society. There was a need for much more education and this ought to begin in primary schools. She argued that there were many types of problem drinker and many different kinds of drinking pattern. Alcohol education should not attempt to discover a single drinking style within a region and address only that. She had been unable to discover a pattern of drinking characteristic of the county and her caseload was extremely diverse.

The community psychiatric nurse was based in the same hospital and worked a specific geographical patch that included Westcross and Lyncombe. The majority of her referrals were from the hospital but a limited number were also accepted from GPs. In recent years she had developed her interest in working with clients with alcohol problems with the support of the consultant psychiatrist. Service provision was excellent at the hospital and by the Council on Alcoholism but greater resources were needed to allow services to develop more generally throughout the county.

Most of the patients seen by this nurse had well established drink problems. The nurse preferred this since it was impossible for the patient to deny there was a problem. At the same time, early detection was needed to prevent problems. GPs needed to become more efficient at recognising alcohol related illness; large firms should be persuaded to develop alcohol recovery programmes. Her caseload was varied but she could not discern any particular drinking patterns. She felt that once someone had become physically damaged by alcohol, it was unlikely that they could or should become a controlled drinker. Most people believed they could and they had to go through this stage. Even 'problem' drinkers who were not physically damaged required about six months of abstinence to enable them to handle drink properly.

With regard to alcohol education, she ran a course at a local comprehensive school which covered all aspects of psychiatric illness. Two or three sessions were devoted to alcohol. Each pupil was asked to keep an alcohol diary; nearly all of them had been drinking since they were 13. She felt young people were under enormous pressure to drink from pubs and from general advertising. The socially acceptable face of alcohol encouraged young people to drink which was not the case with smoking or solvent abuse. One approach to reducing this problem would be more sophisticated advertising for non-alcoholic drinks.

(b)   Health education

The district health education officer (HEO) is centrally concerned with determining health education priorities for her district health authority. There were three other HEOs in her department. One of these specialised in school liaison, one in nurses' education and GP liaison, while the third functioned as a resource officer. The district health education officer had been a member of the Executive Committee of the Council on Alcoholism. Pressure of other work led her to resign; she was at that time involved in the development of a health education certificate at the technical college. She had also felt that the Council needed to become more self reliant and not get so much support from the health authority for activities such as report writing.

Alcohol education had never been seen as a priority area by the health authority. Nevertheless it had established a significant foothold in both the schools programme and nurses' training. In the latter, HEOs no longer provided lectures on individual topics but nurses were encouraged to follow Look after yourself courses which developed the self esteem of participants and so discouraged smoking or excessive drinking. Look after yourself courses have been developed by the Health Education Council and are provided through local tutors who often work within the adult education provision of local authorities.

The health authority had established a drug group, but most members believed that drink was the main problem, especially among young people. However, it was very difficult to know for sure. GPs, health visitors and social workers kept no record of alcohol related problems. If such records were kept then a large proportion of 'normal' families could be monitored for the incidence of drink related problems. Such information could be used to open up a debate about drink in society. She accepted that gaining the interest and concern of the general population was problematic. Two approaches appeared likely to break through this problem. First, information about the level of crime, work accidents and road accidents caused by alcohol might stimulate a debate about the role alcohol should play in people's lives. An attempt should be made to reduce the level of social acceptability of nuisance behaviour caused by drink. She was certain the public would support tougher sentences for drink-driving offences. Second, the Look after yourself approach could be further developed. The district health education officer was certain that most people were eager for information about being healthy. People trained about health issues could pick up questions from local groups and supply them with information, for example on alcohol. Group members could then return to their local communities and pass this information on.

(c)   Schools of nursing

One of the clinical nurse tutors at the department of education at a general hospital in a nearby town had a long standing interest in alcohol education. He had been on a Key Tutor course and wished to raise alcohol issues with nursing students. He would like them to be aware of their own drinking and then hopefully use this knowledge in their working practices. He believed that heavy drinking among young nurses and doctors was accepted in much of the hospital community. It was, therefore, crucial to communicate the importance of moderation in drinking. He had a social model of drink problems since his own nursing experiences had made him aware of people turning to alcohol to cope with loneliness, bereavement or stressful jobs. These patterns of drinking could easily slip into excessive consumption.

However, these aspirations would have to be pursued in a difficult climate. Each school of nursing devised its own curriculum around national minimum guidelines. At the time of the visit by SAUS staff there was no written curriculum but the nurse tutors were soon to hold a meeting to start the process of developing one. However, the respondent expected that at best he would be only able to get a brief mention of alcohol in the curriculum. There was little interest in alcohol issues or problems either in the department of nurse education or the hospital. The only real input on alcohol into nurse education at the moment was through a health education officer.

(d) Primary health care

Two GPs, two community nurses and a health visitor were visited. They were from two GP practices, one in Westcross and the other in Lyncombe. The Westcross GP said he came across few drinking problems and he had encountered only a few alcoholics. One was a tramp who spent most of his time in the bus shelter at the top of the road. One patient had moved away from Westcross; another alcoholic had been in and out of the psychiatric hospital. Drying out and treatment was a waste of time for such people since alcoholics were inadequate personalities. They wasted the time of GPs yet other agencies such as social services were not interested in them. He asked questions about drink only if people came with liver or stomach illnesses. He did not ask depressed people about their drinking; they have to offer the information. He had no knowledge of local drinking patterns since he hardly ever went into a pub. He enjoyed a drink at home and he believed in teaching his children how to drink sensibly. He was not concerned about binge drinking by teenagers since they would grow out of it. This process was more problematic for "the lower social class echelons" because they are slow to learn and difficult to help. He agreed that doctors drank heavily when training but this was only a temporary stage apart from those with personality problems.

He was keen that young people should receive better education about alcohol as part of their general learning about health and social skills. He was opposed to stricter laws on availability or increased price levels. The 18 year old rule was bound to be broken and so was pointless. He had experienced prohibition rules in Saudi Arabia and yet everyone seemed to drink. High prices would encourage home brewing. It needed to be appreciated that alcohol and other drugs such as Valium did reduce stress levels and enabled people to relax. If they enabled people to cope with life, their availability should not be restricted.

The second GP was based at Lyncombe and represented the Family Practitioners Committee of the county on the Executive Committee of the Council on Alcoholism. He stressed the need to distinguish between long standing local families and more recent newcomers in any consideration of illness and drinking patterns. Retirement and redundancy had brought many to Lyncombe - the majority of local tourist businesses were run by newcomers. The diet of long standing families was not healthy - there was too much cream, pastry and fat. The workload at the surgery was high. He felt this reflected the unhealthy diet but also the fact that the surgery was always open and accessible. Arthritis and diabetes seemed particularly common, especially among the older residents.

This GP had always been aware of a small minority in the village with a drink problem. However, for many years there was nothing to offer them in terms of treatment. Psychiatrists refused to help - there was no Council on Alcoholism. Now he could refer to the main psychiatric hospital or the Council. He had helped recently with two home detoxifications. Two of his patients, both women, had liver damage from drinking. Others should have experienced such damage considering their drinking careers, but they had seemed to avoid physical harm. He believed regular drinking rather than binge drinking put people more at risk from liver cirrhosis. However, a binge could often trigger off a stroke. He was not convinced that it could be proved that drink was a significant causal factor in large amounts of heart disease, cancers and stomach problems.

Overall, drink was not a great problem in his community. Local people make little use of pubs. These were full in the summer with tourists but virtually empty for the rest of the year. One would hardly ever find more than five locals in a pub.

Three aspects of drinking caused this GP most concern. He was worried that many mothers at home drifted into patterns of heavy drinking through isolation. Second, he felt that teenagers were being encouraged to drink more and at an early age because of the glamorous advertising of alcohol. Third, he believed there was a need to tackle stress at work since this often led to heavy drinking. This was true of both doctors and fishermen.

He felt alcohol education should concentrate upon the young. It should accept that most of them will drink. He agreed with the "Stay low" message from the Ministry of Transport at Christmas 1984, which he felt was more realistic than "Don't drink and drive". He believed parents should take their children to pubs and teach them how to drink sensibly. He was less sure of the role of staff at GP practices. Midwives had a role in stressing the dangers of smoking and alcohol to pregnant women. GPs, health visitors and nurses were involved with crisis work, not prevention. GPs had no incentive to do more preventive work since they were not paid for it.

The two community nurses and the health visitor were from the Westcross practice. They were in agreement that it was rare to come across people with drinking problems in their work. The occasional alcoholic would be referred to AA. Patients were not asked questions about drinking in relation to problems such as bereavement or depression. The health visitor stressed that the diet of those 'born and bred' in the county was much more of a problem. It was high in sugar and fat. Diabetes and circulatory illnesses were very widespread. All of them said that such people might often be overweight, but they were not heavy drinkers. The community nurse who was born in the county stressed that this was because of the Methodist principles of local people. The attitudes of people who were born in the county were different from those of 'foreigners' or 'incomers'. They do not drink in the home. Local people liked to save their money and not spend it on drink. The only problem was the influence of 'incomers' who undermined the culture of the county. They drank both at home and regularly in pubs. This type of influence encouraged under age drinking and addiction to drink.

The other two respondents confirmed that there was considerable hostility to 'foreigners'. They also stressed how informal social contact in small communities helped to monitor and reduce excessive drinking and under age drinking. At the same time, one of them had encountered problems of teenage binge drinking at a party for her teenage daughter; this behaviour had not been restricted to the children of 'incomers'. All three agreed that social clubs and working men's clubs were important in the Westcross area. Youngsters would enter as guests of parents or older siblings. This often led to under age drinking.

The two nurses said that most people drank to socialise but a minority drank in order to cope with personality problems. It was an addiction that some people were more prone to than others. The health visitor said she thought a problem drinker was someone who had a drink every day or who needed a drink in the morning. She believed that many people experienced a stage of heavy drinking, but that the majority learnt by experience. People behaved in this way when they had no responsibilities. When married, money was used for other things; it was needed for the necessities of life rather than the frivolities.

Finally, all three stressed the relative affluence of Westcross and linked this to the main employer. This firm paid high wages and it subsidised a large number of community facilities and activities. The nurse who had been born in the county was particularly enthusiastic about how this included financial support for numerous village festivals that helped to keep alive the local way of life. The director and senior managers of this firm were like the old squires who provided for sick and elderly people in their communities.

Counselling services and alcohol education

(a)   Statutory agencies

One probation officer from the Westcross office had been on a Key Tutor course and was co-runner of an alcohol education group with an MSC funded member of the Council on Alcoholism. This officer had been sent on the Key Tutor course by her chief probation officer (CPO) as training to run this group. This CPO was on the Executive Committee of the Council on Alcoholism.

The alcohol education group had been in operation since January 1985. It was not designed for alcohol dependent clients, but rather probation clients at an earlier drinking stage who nevertheless had drink related offending patterns or drink related personal problems. Each group of clients received eight sessions which attempted to educate participants about the damage alcohol can cause. The client was seen as then having to make his or her own decision about stopping drinking or how to limit consumption. Some of these clients might volunteer to attend but the majority would have this group listed as a specified activity in a non custodial court sentence. Attendance at the group could also be made a condition of an early release licence from detention centre. A typical case would be an 18 year old with three drink related convictions, one for criminal damage and two for assault.

She felt that probation clients often misused drink. Her colleagues in the office had made a rough estimate that 40% of clients had a drink problem or had become involved in crime after drinking. Young people who were unemployed or on low wages would go for a weekend drinking binge. Such a binge might involve a litre of home brew followed by eight large cans of strong lager. They then got involved in vandalism, assault, abusive words and motoring offences. Other drugs seemed insignificant in Westcross.

Despite the above comments, she felt heavy drinking was just a phase for most people. It might cause some physical harm but it was a part of growing up. Large numbers of young people might get into trouble with the police but the majority would marry and settle down. However, the odd heavy drinker carried on 'out of control' and created enormous difficulties for family and friends. Such patterns of behaviour tended to repeat themselves in families but she did not know whether this was a reflection of 'nature' or 'nurture'. Such individuals were weak. This weakness was possibly learnt from parents but it might be a latent genetic problem or disease.

Some people were doomed to alcoholism and very heavy drinking. There was little that alcohol education could do for this group. Therefore, education initiatives should not focus on those most 'at risk' but rather attempt to increase knowledge of the general population about the physiological effects of alcohol. These views led her to feel some anxiety about likely success rates in her alcohol education group. Participants were very heavy drinkers and their patterns of drink were well established. It would be very difficult to change behaviour and attitudes in only eight sessions.

Education for the general population was important but so was the cost imposed by alcoholics on others such as friends, family and employers. More resources were desperately needed for treatment to tackle such problems.

The chief probation officer and assistant chief probation officer were based in an office in a nearby town. As already indicated, the former was a member of the Executive Committee of the Council on Alcoholism and instigator of the alcohol education group. He explained that the motivation for the group came from several

104

sources. They were aware of similar experiments in other parts of the country. Probation officers were expressing concern about the number of their clients involved in the misuse of alcohol. Magistrates complained that little was being done for the 17-21 year olds who got involved in criminal activity as a result of weekend drinking. A quick survey of 100 social enquiry reports suggested that 40% of court cases had a drink element. The director of the Council on Alcoholism was enthusiastic about establishing a new group and offered to help with staffing. The project had so far struggled to generate sufficient members, partly because magistrates were proving reluctant to accept suggestions that attendance at the group represented an appropriate punishment.

Despite the perceived need for the group, these probation officers did not feel that the county had a large drink problem, especially when compared to other parts of the country. Many young people went to discos and pubs because there was nowhere else to go. However, the amount of drink consumed remained modest, partly because of the influence of Methodism especially in the villages, and partly from informal social control in the villages. The police made little effort to prosecute under age drinkers. Drinking in the county took place in the context of a high tolerance of authority, reflected in compliance with paying fines and low levels of trade union activity. Such attitudes helped people to cope with life, despite low incomes which have been historically a characteristic of the region. There was not the same feeling of the need to catch up economically as there would be in many urban areas. Local people were relaxed and felt little need to drink. The main anxiety of these officers in the area of alcohol was the growth of drink and driving offences in the county.

The social services office in Westcross has two child care teams and one social care team. One of the social workers interviewed was the principal officer for the whole office; the other was a member of the child care team that covered Westcross. The child care social worker said he had only three teenagers in the last 12 months who had committed offences when drunk. One had committed an assault, one had been involved in theft, and the other had been involved in both assault and theft. Both felt that most young people go through a binge phase as part of the process of growing up. Only a few get into trouble with the police and they were the more disturbed and vulnerable. Most of them came from 'established problem families'. Apart from these families, there were no great drink problems in Westcross. It was difficult to help the 'problem families' because they were not susceptible to education. One of the social workers had attended a drug abuse seminar for parents at a local comprehensive school. The parents with children 'at risk' had not turned up.

Neither of them felt this perceived moderation in drinking in Westcross was because of Methodism. Westcross was a cosmopolitan town because of the influence of tourism and the major employer. The principal officer claimed that Westcross was a placid place. There were no 'louts' throwing stones through windows and the public was not worried by a small amount of quiet under age drinking. Unemployment had not grown sufficiently to change this situation. Even young people on the Youth Training Scheme still got permanent jobs at the end of their 12 months. Their office dealt with the 'unemployables' who could not cope with jobs even if they were offered. For this group, child abuse and family violence evolved out of a complex mix of personal weaknesses, low incomes, poor housing and long term unemployment. Such parents had a history of unhappy childhood, instability and borstal. These problems started well before any possible heavy drinking and so drink itself was not an important factor as an explanatory variable for subsequent social problems.

Both social workers said they enjoyed a drink and both drank at home; they believed in teaching their children how to drink sensibly. The child care social worker said that the drink and drive laws in such a rural county reduced pub drinking. Local people could not afford to lose their licences; he never drank and drove. The other said he still had a drink when driving and that he was perfectly safe; he had had a licence for 30 years and never had an accident.

(b)   Voluntary agencies

The nearest Samaritans' office was 14 miles away and they felt a meeting would not be worthwhile. They had no data or views about alcohol related issues. They suspected many of their clients had alcohol problems, but this was often a secondary response to a traumatic event such as redundancy, bereavement or divorce. The Samaritans saw themselves as a listening post. They were not experts on particular issues and they did not pressurise clients to contact other agencies against their will. They had no views about existing treatment services or alcohol education.

Two marriage guidance counsellors were seen. The office of the Marriage Guidance Council for the county is based in Westcross in the same building as the Council on Alcoholism. Both organisations are allowed to use these premises rent free by the owner who is the major employer in the town. The service covers the whole of the county and there are 12 counsellors and an administrator. In January 1985, 107 cases were seen for marital counselling and 32 cases for sex therapy. These clients tended to be skilled working class or middle class people. The service depended upon clients verbalising their feelings and this came more naturally for some groups than others.

Both stressed the complexity of the relationship between drink and marriage difficulties. If drink turned out to be the dominant problem for one partner and the other agreed, they might be referred to the Council on Alcoholism. However, most clients self-selected themselves for marriage guidance. They wanted their marriage to be the focus of intervention. For many, heavy drinking seemed to begin when the marriage started to face difficulties; it was a method of coping with the resultant pressure. Drinking would probably decline if this pressure was reduced through conciliation or divorce. They did have cases where the wives of drinking husbands needed support. However, they had to be careful about challenging people about their drinking. Clients came to the Marriage Guidance Council about their marriage and not for counselling on drink. Clients had to be given time to make their own decision about the nature of their problems. Even where heavy drinking was well established, one had to ask why. What caused it? What were the underlying anxieties? The counsellors were inclined to focus on how relationship difficulties led on to heavy drinking. They felt Councils on Alcoholism tended to abstract out drink as the key variable. Communication problems were by far the most common difficulty that they had to address. However, unemployment was a growing issue; it led to loss of self-esteem in the husband and loss of respect from the wife.

Neither felt drinking patterns in Westcross were a cause for concern. Heavy drinkers were excluded from the sex therapy courses; only one in 107 applicants had been turned down for this reason. People in a rural county needed cars and motorbikes to get about. They had to be careful of the drink and drive laws. They both felt children should be taught how to drink socially rather than see it as a taboo to be broken. Westcross was an affluent town which had outgrown itself. The town centre was 'dead' in the evenings. Residents drank in the pubs and clubs in the villages which had been swallowed up in the outward expansion of the town.

Marriage Guidance Councils had been heavily influenced by theorists such as Carl Rogers.[4] These theorists stressed that clients needed space to explore their own problems and develop their own solutions. Healing would evolve from this. Supplying Drinkwatch material or talking about controlled drinking was inconsistent with this non-directive philosophy and it deflected clients away from the main reason for coming. However, there was a debate about whether this approach needed to be amended. Some counsellors were now offering concrete choices to clients. The sex therapy sessions were designed to modify behaviour. The national training syllabus had just been updated and now contained more sessions focused on social factors which influence and inform the lives of clients.[5]

(c)   The churches

Two Methodist ministers were contacted but both refused to talk to the research team. The first asked to be sent information about the programme and the research. She was re-contacted after this was sent. She said she had no particular knowledge or views to offer on alcohol treatment or alcohol education. However, she would ask whether the Fraternal Meeting, which was held weekly between all denominations, would be willing to talk to the research team. A further telephone call suggested they were not interested. At the briefing conference for the South West alcohol education programme in April 1985 it was suggested that another minister might be more interested. However, he conveyed the same views but with more hostility. The Fraternity had to pick up the pieces from drink problems and they had no desire to sit around just talking about the issues.

Alcohol and the education department

(a)   Schools

The county education department does not have an adviser whose main responsibility is pastoral education, social education or health education. It was not discovered until towards the end of the fieldwork that the physical education adviser also takes responsibility for health education. This officer was not seen. However, she was a member of a teacher working group on health education that had been attempting to increase the coverage of health education issues in the county schools. This working group evolved out of a county conference in 1981 which reflected the desire of the authority to see a greater emphasis on work in this area. The conference was partly a reflection of DHSS pressure on local authorities to emphasise to young people the need for self responsibility for health in which everyone would be encouraged to take adequate exercise, reduce stress and tension, eat balanced meals, stop smoking and use alcohol in moderation.[6]

The working party established from the conference produced a report on Health Education in the schools of the county in September 1983. This report argued for a co-ordinated approach to health education for both primary and secondary schools. Health education was perceived as a lifelong process in which young people need continuing help and guidance in decision making and relationship forming skills. Health education in secondary schools was seen as having six main aims:

(a)   To promote self-awareness and develop self-esteem (if you do not respect yourself as a person you will find it difficult to establish successful relationships with other people, where it is essential to respect their feelings).

(b)   To provide knowledge about the biological, emotional and social aspects of human development and to foster the kind of understanding necessary for leading a healthy, responsible and harmonious life.

(c)   To develop the decision making skills about behaviour which are essential to maintain physical and mental well-being in a rapidly changing society.

(d)   To help pupils feel responsible for their own health related behaviour and care about the effect of their behaviour on others.

(e)   To develop an understanding of inter-personal relationships and the skills to manage relationships with others.

(f)   To develop respect for individual rights and moral values.

It was explained that a co-ordinated approach could be achieved in one of four ways, namely an integrated system across subject areas, a separate course, a pastoral system or a combination of the three. The preference of the working party for the integrated system was clear and the following example (Table 15) was given of how this could be tackled in relation to alcohol education.

However, the report also discussed some of the obstacles to achieving a co-ordinated approach to health education in county schools. It was difficult to find space for new developments in the existing curriculum. Staff might feel uneasy about tackling sensitive issues or using small group teaching techniques, and that health education was 'poaching' on their territory, if parts of their subject were allocated to a separate course; they might resent being asked to give up time from their subject and question the availability of resources.

Discussions were held with one member of the working party. She taught biology, health education and child care at a comprehensive school in a small seaside town which was 10 miles from Westcross. The health education curriculum at the school was based on an integrated system. Biology and chemistry in the second year looked at yeast and how wine could be produced. Alcohol was distilled and its potency measured. This was a purely factual input. In the fourth year attitudes could begin to be addressed. Home economics taught which wines were appropriate for which meals. How to order wine in a restaurant was explained. However, this teacher had just left and would not be replaced because of shrinking pupil numbers. The fourth year also saw the beginning of the main health education syllabus which had several alcohol education elements. In Run for your life, the body was drawn and life support mechanisms listed. Dangers to these systems were listed, and one of these was the danger to the liver of alcohol. Under Stereotypes, attractive and unattractive forms of behaviour were discussed in small groups. One stereotype considered was the drunk; drunken men were far more acceptable to the pupils than drunken women. In Free to choose, several sessions were organised around the BBC programmes on drinking.

However, much of the syllabus made no specific mention of drink. Children soon reacted against too much focus on one area. The course looked at how social rules, peer group pressures and advertising pressures influenced lifestyle in areas such as diet and smoking. Pupils tended to be fascinated more by illegal drugs than legal drugs.

Throughout the health education work, a key component was the general health education questionnaire developed by John Balding at the HEC Schools Health Education Unit, Exeter University.[7] This was a mechanism for describing the actual behaviour of pupils and provided a pivotal point for small group and class discussions. It avoided the adoption of a prescriptive approach. The starting point was actual behaviour and attitudes, and the first question was

Table 15:   An integrated approach to alcohol education in schools

Facts: Knowledge component of alcohol education

Activities

Biology
Chemistry

Experiments to produce alcohol from fermenting fruit or vegetable juices. Distillation of home made wine and beer to find the percentage alcohol by volume. Drawing on graphs, charts, posters showing the alcohol of commercial beers, wines, spirits. Information about the effects of blood alcohol levels on the body and the effects of long term alcohol abuse.

Attitudes to drinking

Activities

Health education
Religious education
English
Social studies

Examination of stereotypes often associated with alcohol and dispelling myths concerning alcoholic men and women, teetotallers, the drunk driver, people who drink to impress others. Pupils explore their own feelings through discussion and drama. Examination of alcohol advertising to discover the messages implicit in the advertisements eg drinking improves social status, increases number of friends, degree of strength and attractiveness of drinker.

Pressures to drink and situation in which to drink

Activities

Home economics

Planning special occasion meals and parties where alcohol is available, using alcohol in cooking. Moderate use of alcohol in the home.

English
Health education
Social studies
Human biology

Examination of media, social and peer pressures in alcohol use. Examination of stressful situations and alcohol use/abuse. Social statistics on alcohol abuse.

why? The overall aim was to enable young people to make their own health and lifestyle decisions.

This teacher also supplied her own views about drinking patterns among young people in her part of the county. Young people drank early in her community. By 15 they had already been on a binge and been really ill. By 18 they were much more sensible. By 20 they were controlled drinkers. One reason for this was that local people were child centred and yet young people were given freedom to explore. Pubs let in children and this had general community acceptance because it was somewhere to meet. Young people mature early in the county and they do this in the security of caring families. As a result, there was a mixture of freedom to drink combined with social control to restrict abuse.

She stressed that schools in the county varied enormously in their enthusiasm for health education. It all depended on the presence of a committed teacher and/or an interested head teacher. The present climate was not conducive to a growth in health education. Schools were under enormous pressure to respond to so many different initiatives such as profiling, the push for better science teaching and the 16+ exam. Staff morale was low because of falling rolls, low wages and industrial action. The health education group no longer met regularly.

Another member of this health education group was also visited. She was a health education co-ordinator at a comprehensive school six miles from Westcross. The schools serviced numerous villages to the West of Westcross. She outlined the health education syllabus for the third to fifth years. In the third year, the focus was on health and fitness with a special emphasis on smoking and prevention of heart disease. In the fourth year, there were three modules of work, namely drug addiction and alcohol, safety issues and sex education. The focus in the fifth year was on preparing for work, social services, leisure, and law and order. The questionnaire developed by John Balding had been used once, but it did not appear to influence the content of this part of the course. The teacher stressed her support for the message that drink in moderation was fine, especially if part of normal social life. At the same time, drink did not solve problems but only led to further complications. The course material and text books, however, seemed to focus more narrowly on the 'alcoholic', and how his disease could be treated.

This teacher felt there were few drinking problems in the locality. The rural parts of the county tended to be behind the rest of the country in terms of lifestyle. Alcohol consumption was no exception. Under age drinking was common in local pubs but this provoked little interest from parents or the police. Such drinking occurred typically in the village 'local' where the child and his parents were well known. This teacher would like to see licensing hours relaxed to become more like the continent with a greater focus on family drinking. Methodist parents would oppose such a development, but it was their children who tended to present problems.

The school still operated in a relatively buoyant local labour market. All but the real hard core of low achievers found employment on leaving school. Employment was dominated by the main employer, especially in mining, the county council, commerce, tourism and the army. YTS entrants were finding permanent employment after their trainee year.

Discussions were also held with five teachers from the two comprehensives and the sixth form college in Westcross. The teacher at one of these comprehensive schools was responsible for an Education for life module in the fourth and fifth years, which was based on an old social studies course used when the school was still a grammar. The aim of the course was to explore values for life and then to allow pupils to make their own decisions. Alcohol was addressed in some sessions through the use of Tacade materials while AA speakers were also used. This teacher was not convinced that the school was tackling this area of work in an effective way. There were two main problems. The Education for life module did not lead to an exam, and so had low status within the school. Most teachers were not confident in tackling sensitive issues or handling group discussions.

The catchment area of the second comprehensive school was the Southern half of Westcross and Southern villages, including Lyncombe. The deputy headmistress and home economics teacher explained that the school had no specific course on skills for life or health education. The focus of teaching was in enabling young people to pass examinations. Alcohol was mentioned as part of the 'O' level child care and development course: this was taken by girls only. The effect of alcohol on the body was covered in third year science teaching. A speaker was known to have been used from the Western Temperance League. There was a consensus among staff that children needed to know the effect of alcohol, but there was confusion and anxiety about what overall message was most appropriate. Media presentation of alcohol meant that a 'don't drink' message would be ignored, yet they were afraid of upsetting Methodist or temperance families if they approached the subject in any other way. The mentioning of topics such as alcohol and sex might give pupils ideas and lead to increased experimentation.

The sixth form college of 500 pupils served several local comprehensives. The two tutors said there was a compulsory general studies course with a variety of optional elements. The central element of the course was preparation for 'moving on' (eg filling in forms, job interviews etc). A number of outside speakers such as the Samaritans and the drug squad did sessions on the course. They were not sure whether alcohol education was mentioned but they were sure that the sixth form college only 'tinkered' in this area. This might be about to change because their headmaster wished to make use of Tacade materials on drinking. The course often received criticism from pupils partly because it did not reflect the input on Education for life type courses that many pupils had already received prior to arriving at the college. College teachers did not know how to tackle alcohol education. It was wrong to ignore the problem yet there was also the danger of glamourising misuse, so that one encouraged drinking among those not previously interested. Some pupils were beyond the point where warnings of drink would be useful.

The level of anxiety in the above comments reflected the impact of a row about pupil drinking in the previous year. The police had complained about the growth of pupil drinking at lunchtime in the town centre. All college pupils had been warned of the possible consequences of any continuance of this behaviour. The rules of the college suggested expulsion was the appropriate punishment but there was uncertainty about whether the education authority would support this. Things had seemed to quieten down since the warning. These tutors felt that village pubs were often 'seedy' and used by what they called "the more dubious elements" such as local 'roughs' or visitors from other towns. The older 'respectable' residents drank in social clubs. Drinking by college pupils was most likely to happen at home or in discos, such as the one run by the rugby club. The college did run socials with 'live' music. Drinking on the premises was not allowed, but many pupils visited the pub before arrival. The tutors did not believe that Methodism was still an influence on local drinking patterns.

The teacher at the first comprehensive school claimed that there were 'tremendous drink problems' in Westcross. She believed children bought bottles from supermarkets or used the drinks cupboard of their parents. Occasional situations did arise in which pupils were unable to function properly at school because of the amount of alcohol consumed the night before. She felt that some experimentation was inevitable given the level of peer group and advertising pressure. At the same time, alcohol abuse needed to be checked and challenged. This was a factor in setting up a Use and abuse of drugs seminar for parents which emphasised the centrality of drink. However, the parents were interested only in illegal drugs. The teachers at the other school emphasised their lack of knowledge of drinking patterns amongst their pupils. They heard gossip about lax landlords and the large late night disco centre. They experienced disquiet when a pupil entered a pub where they were drinking but these were usually known troublemakers. They concentrated upon ensuring that no alcohol was consumed on school premises.

(b)   The youth service

The education department of the county employs six area youth officers, one for each of the district councils. The area youth officer who covers the district which includes Westcross said his role was to offer support to all the various voluntary youth clubs in his area, most of which were open one or two nights per week with volunteer help. He also helped to supervise two full time youth leaders who were seconded to voluntary organisations by the local authority.

He said that most youth clubs had a drinking problem, especially when they ran a disco. The problem was that young people had often been drinking before they arrived. However, he did not feel any great concern about this. Parents were now more lax and some pubs geared themselves to the young drinker. More drink was now kept in the home. Drink remained a one night a week event for young people. They go on a weekend binge and put themselves at risk. Disposable cash was short. Wages were low yet house prices and the cost of living were high. There were rarely any gang fights or real trouble in Westcross as a result of teenage drinking. It was inevitable that young people would experiment with drink. The discussion of sensible drinking by schools might help but there was always a danger that this would only serve to encourage participation by more youngsters. In any case, pubs provided the only reasonable meeting place for most young people in the county.

Youth clubs were usually open only one evening a week and run from draughty and dilapidated village halls.

The full time youth worker based in a large seaside resort took a very different view. Most young people drank far too much. They did not understand the effects of alcohol on the body and they drank it like coke. Young people were encouraged strongly to drink at home as early as 13 or 14 years old. They then started to buy alcohol from supermarkets and by 16 and 17 they were drinking in pubs. Police needed to crack down on such under age drinking but they just ignored the problem. Parents were too busy in the summer with tourism to supervise their children. Heavy drinkers stayed clear of his club because they knew he would not tolerate drinking. He wished to see the availability of drink greatly reduced and licensing laws on age and opening hours rigidly enforced. He felt the present lax attitude of the police was a disgrace.

The second full time youth worker was based in a club in Westcross. This purpose built centre was based on a coffee bar/disco principle rather than on the provision of good indoor sports facilities or rooms for small groups. At first everything was fine. Rock bands played, discos were held and 450 people would turn up. However, a recreation centre has now been opened, a late night disco became established and several public houses began to gear themselves to the youth market. Village youngsters can no longer get back from the town at night because of the lack of evening buses. Membership collapsed and left a hard core of 'roughs' who used the Friday night disco as a venue for a fight after heavy drinking at local pubs. Some of the volunteer helpers had up to nine pints before they arrived. The club had got a bad name and many parents would have nothing to do with it. The club was in financial trouble and the building needed substantial repairs.

The present leader had been there for only six months and was trying to tackle these problems. The worst troublemakers had now been banned. In general, he felt most people in Westcross were law abiding and did not drink to excess. Schoolchildren from the local comprehensives hardly ever got into trouble. However, there was a stratum of manual workers in the county who thought that men had to be hard and that one way to prove this was to drink hard. Such attitudes were prevalent among many miners, who would drink several pints every night in their social and working men's clubs. He felt Methodism had no influence on drinking patterns.

(c) Colleges of further education

Five lecturers from the large college of further education in Westcross were visited. One was head of liberal studies and the others taught sociology, biology/nursing studies, psychology and English/liberal studies. The college had 11,000 students, over 1,000 day release or part time students and 3,000 evening class participants. There were 110 full time equivalent teaching posts.

There was no indication that alcohol education featured strongly in the curricula of these various subjects, most of which were taught to 'A' level standard. Sociology looked at youth subcultures and this included a consideration of illegal drugs but not alcohol. The biology and nursing students were offered the basic facts about alcohol. They were seen as having the right to choose their own drinking patterns. Nurses were very interested in the whole area of drugs and society. The psychology lecturer said that his students were far more interested in issues relating to illegal drugs. The English and liberal studies lecturer had a general interest in lifestyle and how this was reflected in diet and attitudes to health. However, alcohol did not seem an important area, especially to female students who made little use of public houses. The head of liberal studies stressed there was no college or departmental policy on topics such as alcohol education.   It depended on the requirements of each syllabus and the interest of lecturers. In general, he felt colleges were under pressure to tackle and address too many social problems. It was in danger of stopping any real teaching for 'A' level.

Staff were in agreement that students created few problems or worries in relation to drink. The lecturers drank far more than the students, who tended to lack money. Students only drank heavily on special occasions such as an 18th birthday, Christmas or after exams. Three of the lecturers had 10 teenage children between them. All had been taught how to drink socially. They were all moderate drinkers. All were agreed that under age drinking was common in the county but that early entry to public houses reduced later binge drinking. The pub was a meeting place and was treated with respect. The sociology lecturer said that a recent visit to court with students made her realise the frequency of drink related crime in Westcross.

Alcohol and the law

(a)   The police

The police inspector at the Westcross police station was able to provide only very limited data on alcohol related offences and these statistics referred to the whole of the police authority rather than the Westcross area.   This information is, nevertheless, summarised in Table 16. He also said that there had been 2,133 notified road accidents in 1984. The most common cause listed was going too fast (339 cases).   Alcohol was the fourth main contributory cause and this accounted for 124 of the accidents.

Table 16:   Alcohol related offences in the police authority

Year	Prosecutions for excess alcohol when breathalysed	No. of breathalyser tests given	Convictions for drunkenness and drunk/ disorderly
1982	1,787	4,788	1,193
1983	2,399	7,160	1,395
1984	2,657	6,554	N/A

The police inspector said it was very difficult to judge the volume of drink related crime. If police resources were directed to uncover alcohol related crime, then this would be found and alcohol related offences would appear to increase.   The inspector had recently moved from a large city and he stressed the difference between the two areas. In the city many outlets were in the centre and these were away from residential areas.   There were few complaints about noise. However, people go on to clubs from the pubs. They drift into binge drinking. The sheer volume of drinks leads to stupid behaviour.   Violence and theft were a massive problem. Little of this existed in Westcross. Here the problem flowed from the closeness of many pubs and clubs to residential areas. Local residents complained about noise but little else.

He confirmed that town centre pubs in Westcross were busy only at lunchtime.   Local people drank in their residential areas and villages in the evening. Under age drinking did exist. The sixth form college had had to crack down on lunchtime drinking. All his police sergeants were allocated specific public houses to visit on a regular basis. However, the need for allocation reflected the fact that such monitoring was seen as a low priority relative to other aspects of police work. Responsibility had to be allocated to individuals if this task was not to be overlooked. Youngsters in the county were not rich and did not drink a great deal. Family rooms in pubs were common. Young people entered pubs with parents at an early age and they learnt how to behave and drink sensibly in public houses.

He expressed his enthusiasm for alcohol education and he had enjoyed his participation on a Key Tutor course. He had been recommended for the course by his chief superintendent since he was expected to move into training rather than into his present post in Westcross. However, he felt that it was very problematic to introduce such ideas as alcohol education into police training. Most policemen were interested in alcohol only in so far as it led to crime. Policemen saw themselves as crime detectors rather than involved in prevention. Helping the criminal was the job of the court or 'do-gooders'. Most policemen were not interested in whether they could or should refer to the helping agencies. He felt such attitudes were narrow and wrong, yet they were dominant and difficult to challenge. Training officers would soon get rejected if they went too far.

The police constable at Lyncombe had been stationed there for twelve years but was about to leave. He did not see his community as having many drinking problems. There were about ten very heavy drinkers and these tended to be about 40 years old and single. Theft and criminal damage sometimes happened after leaving the pub, but the culprit was usually easy to find in such a small community. Heavy drinking took place on Friday and Saturday nights when the fishing boats were in harbour. He did agree that 16 and 17 year olds were often to be found in pubs. He was more worried, however, by situations in which men returned home from the pub and became involved in marital violence; the drinking session might have been sparked off by domestic tensions in the first place. However, these situations were virtually impossible to interfere with because of traditional beliefs about sorting out one's own problems.

He felt the community was quite contradictory in some of its attitudes. Methodism remained strong amongst older residents. There was plenty of work in fishing and tourism but house prices were beyond the reach of many locals. Tourism brought permissive attitudes and local girls were always getting pregnant. It was a suspicious community and it would be hostile to any alcohol education campaign from outsiders.

(b)   Magistrates

The chairman of the bench for the local magistrates' court expressed disquiet with the chaotic nature of licensing hours. He had managed to achieve a uniform pattern of licensing hours with the nearest bench and this should stop boundary hopping to get a late drink. He was unhappy about the growth in registered club and late night licences.   At the same time, he thought there was something to be said for a more continental approach because criminal behaviour seemed more associated with drink when access was restricted.

He was very concerned about the volume of alcohol related crime especially in the areas of theft and grievous bodily harm. He had estimated that 80% of indictable offences in his sessional area over the past three years had been related to excessive consumption of alcohol.   About four cases per week concern drink and driving offences.   He had omitted known alcoholics from these figures because they had an illness and could not be considered normal people. Alcohol was a far bigger problem than illegal drugs. Some young people were drinking ten pints of cider a night. He found AA to be the most useful helping agency.   The young unemployed seemed most 'at risk'. It was essential that schools tackled alcohol education in a thorough manner.   Young people needed to understand the effect of alcohol on the body, and how to use alcohol in a sensible way as part of normal social life.

Miscellaneous

(a)   The Youth Training Scheme

The Youth Training Scheme was established by the Manpower Services Commission in 1983 as a one year basic training for all 16 year old school leavers who wanted to participate. YTS was split into two modes of delivery. Under Mode A, a managing agent - an employer or group of employers - took responsibility for the complete programme of a group of trainees. On the other hand, the Mode B method of delivery was, in effect, where the MSC acted as the managing agency and then subcontracted out responsibility for the various elements. Mode B has tended to be characterised as being for 'disadvantaged' young people who are not ready for the world of work.[8]

The main employer in Westcross runs the largest YTS scheme in the county. Four hundred trainees were recruited in the first year, 580 in the second, and they hoped to find up to 600 in the third. The manager of this scheme explained that placements were not restricted to the premises of this firm. Trainees were placed in small businesses such as garages and hairdressers throughout much of the county. Each business was called a sponsor but it remained the responsibility of the managing agent to monitor progress. Few applicants were turned away. They were rejected for Mode A only if they were seen as not ready for the world of work; in this case, they were directed to the nearest Mode B scheme.

50% of the 13 week 'off the job training' was provided by a college of further education and 50% by the firm. There was also an equal time split between sessions devoted to learning practical skills and those spent on life and social skills. However, he felt that trainees only learnt the latter if such teaching was grounded in practical tasks. They also faced restrictions from sponsors. They once let a group of young people 'cost' food at the local supermarket because they seemed so unaware of the real price of food. Many sponsors were furious. They thought it was a frivolous waste of time and was irrelevant to work performance. The YTS manager felt there was little scope for addressing issues such as alcohol education because of these pressures. At the moment, there was just a half day given over to health education issues in the induction week. This session was run by the occupational health nurse.

He believed that young people in the county tended to be moderate drinkers. Tourists were a bad influence in the summer, especially in the major seaside resort. There was sometimes fighting at discos between local youth and young holidaymakers. He felt rural life encouraged maturity, including sensible patterns of drinking. At the end of the induction week, trainees were asked to fill out a Know yourself questionnaire which had two questions on drinking. The first of these asked the trainees what they drank and the second asked how much they drank. The research team were allowed to collate this material and the results are presented in Tables 17 and 18. The information of the trainees was converted into 'units' by the research team in which one unit is equivalent to half a pint of beer, one measure of spirits, or a glass of wine or sherry.

Table 17: Alcohol consumption and YTS trainees

No. of units consumed per week	No. of respondents	Male	Female	Sex unknown
Over 30 units	3	3	-	-
21-30 units	8	7	1	-
10-20 units	48	29	19	-
Under 10 units	170	94	76	-
Do not drink alcohol	114	54	60	-
No information	87	38	24	25
TOTALS	430	225	180	25

Table 18: Main alcoholic drink of YTS trainees

Type of drink	Number of repondents
Lager	102
Bitter	38
Cider	16
Spirits, fortified wine and wine	67
Do not drink alcohol	114
No information	93
TOTAL (Trainees)	430

These data support the evidence from the HEC Schools Health Education Unit[9] that a high percentage of young people in the South West consume alcohol on a regular basis. For 16 year old males in this group it would appear that this is typically two to four pints of lager per week and for young females, it is typically about three glasses of a spirit (Pernod, Bacardi or vodka) and two pints of lager. However, these figures have to be treated with great care. Some trainees may have felt a need to boast of their drinking prowess. Others will have been worried about admitting their under age drinking to their new employer. The replies of trainees do not explain if the drinking occurs in the home, the public house, discos or social clubs. It is impossible to distinguish between the truly occasional drinkers and those that drink small amounts on a regular basis. The conversion of the replies into units required the research team to make more assumptions than is normally acceptable in social research.[10]

(b) Occupational health services

The occupational health doctor and nurse for the main employer explained that the company had an 'unofficial' alcohol policy which had been drawn up with the help of the Council on Alcoholism. This took the form of a set of guidelines which had never been officially approved. Heavy drinking usually became an issue when it led to regular absenteeism. The company treated such behaviour as a medical problem and the individual was treated as medically ill so long as he or she was willing to co-operate. Treatment might include drying out, psychiatric treatment, or referral to the Council on Alcoholism. The occupational health nurse was often involved in counselling workers with drink problems. A failure to co-operate with treatment could lead to the situation being considered a disciplinary problem. The relevant shop steward would be informed and dismissal might follow if the problem was not resolved by the first three written warnings.

Both believed drink problems were widespread, especially in the mining industry. Miners drank a great deal of beer. There were a large number of working men's clubs and local football clubs, most of them serving a very localised area. Many miners worked alone and had difficulty in communicating, even with their families. This introverted personality was common in people who had been born in the county. Such people needed to develop a better capacity to communicate, combined with broader leisure and educational interests. The present narrow introversion encouraged alcohol misuse. There were also problems of alcohol misuse among dock workers where cheap drink could be obtained from the boats, and among the salaried classes especially if they were heavily involved in the middle class club network. Abstinence was the only feasible option for most problem drinkers. They both disliked the term 'alcoholic' since they felt it was stigmatising.

(c) The late night disco

Many respondents mentioned the late night disco attached to a large entertainment hall which was situated on the outskirts of Westcross. The administrator of this complex explained that it had been a struggle to obtain a nightly two o'clock licence from the

Methodist influenced magistrates. At the height of its popularity, the disco was attracting 60,000 customers a year. However, it had slipped downmarket and had started to attract the lower end of the socio-economic scale. It was now being refitted and renamed. The new disco would aim for socially aspiring customers with a high disposable income. The entrance fee would be higher and there would be a membership system that gave entry at reduced cost. This would be an incentive for people to behave and would also enable closer monitoring of troublemakers.

In the old disco, the main drink was draught beer and this accounted for 60% of sales. The average spent in late 1984 was £2.77 per head. On Saturday they took £2.81 per head and on Thursday they made £3.10 per head. Beer was 85p per pint. As indicated by the above figures, their big night was Thursday, which was pay night for mining workers of the main employer. Some of these workers were not very bright and some seemed to enjoy fighting. However, the administrator felt that the overall level of drinking in Westcross was less than for large cities, although modest amounts of drink could reduce social control and lead to fighting. Most fights at the disco were with fists and feet; there had only been four incidents involving glasses. The worst tensions arose when a male holidaymaker approached local girls. The management had imposed an 18 year old and above rule on the disco, but it was still difficult to pick out those much younger. Local parents seemed to tolerate ignorance in their children. They were told nothing about alcohol and tended to abuse it hopelessly at the first opportunity. Local parents often treated the disco as a sinful place. A girl was once assaulted after leaving, and her parents considered this a justifiable punishment from God.

Alcohol education in Westcross/Lyncombe and the South West programme

All respondents were asked if they were aware of the South West alcohol education programme prior to contact from the research team. Table 19 confirms the situation found in the other locality studies. Knowledge of the programme in late 1984 and early 1985 was limited beyond those involved in the Council on Alcoholism or health authority; lack of knowledge was particularly marked within the education department.

Of the 14 who had heard of the programme, nine were staff at the Council on Alcoholism or members of its Executive Committee. In some cases, knowledge of the programme was very detailed and two of this group had been on a Key Tutor course. The knowledge of some members of the Executive Council was less clearcut; they were aware of the existence of the programme but very unsure about its aims or philosophy. One member of the Executive Committee said that she was unaware of the programme. Three of those aware of the programme had developed this knowledge primarily through their involvement on a Key Tutor course. Two of them had been 'volunteered' by their 'bosses', while the other was attempting to develop a long standing interest. One person was a health education officer who has been heavily involved in the South West programme from the outset. She is a member of its planning and monitoring group and she also attended a Key Tutor course. The remaining individual who had heard of the programme worked in the same office as a member of the Executive Committee of the Council on Alcoholism.

The bulk of these meetings took place prior to the public launch of the programme in the county at a briefing conference in April 1985. This conference and subsequent developments may have led to a far wider awareness of the South West alcohol education programme amongst professionals in the Westcross area. The senior youth officer, for example, did receive an invitation to the briefing conference after he was visited by the research team. It will be interesting to note the extent to which this situation has changed, when the research team revisits each respondent in 18 months' time. The programme is faced with an enormous task. If the Council on Alcoholism had not been based in Westcross, the research evidence suggests that knowledge of the programme would have been minimal.

Respondents were also asked if they were sympathetic to the aims of the programme. General attitudes to alcohol education were outlined where appropriate in earlier sections of this report, but it is worth taking a specific look at comments about the programme itself. The fourteen respondents who were already aware of the programme were perhaps the most important in this respect, since they had already given some consideration to it prior to the meeting with researchers. A very mixed response was received from this group. One expressed great enthusiasm for the philosophy and aims of the programme. However, this officer expressed concern that the 'climate' of opinion in the South West might create enormous difficulties. It would be difficult to engage the attention and interest of the general public without shock/horror statistics. There was evidence that the various groups involved in alcohol education in the county would fail to work together effectively. In particular, staff at the Council on Alcoholism were annoyed because they believed their expertise was not being recognised. The South West programme lacked the staff to cover such a wide region.

Those associated with the Council on Alcoholism and other specialist provision did confirm the existence of some antagonism towards the programme. Complaints took a variety of forms. Their expertise and knowledge was not recognised and they needed to have a strong reputation to attract funds. The Council felt it was important that it was recognised as expert in dealing with alcohol issues, and this produced a tension in that the programme's philosophy was that alcohol was everybody's business. They initially believed they were entering into a partnership with the Health Education Council (HEC), but instead they had been patronised. The Key Tutor courses were criticised as superficial and offering Key Tutors little guidance or support on how to run their own courses. Attitudes varied about how the programme should define alcohol education. Some felt that the programme risked trivialising drinking issues through its failure to emphasise the costs of alcohol misuse. Some expressed anxiety that a focus on alcohol education should not be allowed to deflect from the search for resources to provide treatment and counselling services that covered the whole of the county. Services were needed and not more investigation. One member of the Executive Committee expressed little faith in the value or need for any kind of alcohol education programme. The consultant psychiatrist expressed scepticism about the whole emphasis upon local drinking patterns and she doubted if there was such a thing as a regional style of drinking. She was annoyed by the failure to appreciate that an alcohol education programme would generate treatment and counselling queries that might overload limited existing facilities.

Perhaps the main and most common complaint from this group was resentment towards 'outsiders' coming in with preconceived ideas. It made people feel that all the things that they had done counted for nothing. They believed the HEC saw their county not only as having done nothing but incapable of doing anything themselves. These feelings seemed to have emanated from the first main meeting held about the programme in the county in Summer 1984. It could be argued that these difficulties have now been overcome. The briefing conference in April 1985 suggested the Executive Committee of the Council on Alcoholism as the planning mechanism for future county initiatives in relation to the programme. Most delegates were impressed by the paper from the

Table 19: Knowledge of the South West alcohol education programme

Subject area of respondent		Number of respond-ents	Aware of prog-ramme	Unaware of prog-ramme
1. Alcohol and specialist provison in the voluntary sector	a) Council on Alcoholism	5	5	0
	b) Self help groups	1	0	1
2. Alcohol and the NHS	a) The psychiatric service	2	1	1
	b) Health education	1	1	0
	c) School of nursing	1	1	0
	d) Primary health care	5	1	4
3. Counselling services and alcohol education	a) Statutory agencies	5	3	2
	b) Voluntary agencies	3	0	3
	c) The churches	2	0	2
4. Alcohol and the education department	a) Schools	7	0	7
	b) The youth service	3	0	3
	c) Colleges of further education	5	0	5
5. Alcohol and the law	a) Police	2	1	1
	b) Magistrates	1	0	1
6. Miscellaneous		4	1	3
TOTAL		47	14	33

Council which outlined their existing educational activities. Hopefully, previous problems of communication will now be eased and efforts can be concentrated upon maximising the effectiveness of the programme. However, it has to be faced that there might be major disagreements between programme staff and some county 'experts' about the appropriate approach to alcohol education and the extent to which this must always focus itself around the theme of alcohol misuse.

This largely pessimistic view of Key Tutor courses was not shared by the other three participants with whom discussions were held. All had thoroughly enjoyed the course. The nurse tutor found the whole teaching approach very instructive and he hoped to introduce more alcohol education into his nurse training work, although establishing this as a priority area with his colleagues would be problematic. He was perhaps the most enthusiastic respondent about the philosophy of the programme. The police inspector enjoyed the course but did not feel it could be applied to police refresher courses for reasons already outlined. The probation officer found the techniques of teaching to be excellent and a great help in the running of her present alcohol education programme. However, she doubted if she would have had the time to form a group to apply this knowledge, if one had not already been waiting for her. In general, she felt that education should be less of a priority than helping problem drinkers and their families with counselling and treatment.

Drinking patterns and problems in Westcross and Lyncombe

The majority of professionals in this study stressed that there was no drink problem in the community. A variety of explanations were given for this - these included lack of money, the 'maturity' of local residents, informal social control in a well established community, the need to protect one's driving licence and Methodism. A few respondents did not share this view and this was especially true in the discussions with members of the Council on Alcoholism who emphasised the generality of alcohol misuse in society. Others stressed that the local mining industry was associated with high levels of alcohol consumption, especially in social clubs. Some 'incomers' to the county stressed that such patterns of behaviour were associated with the type of local long standing resident who was 'strong in the arm and thick in the head'. On the other hand, those 'born and bred' in the county were more inclined to blame any growth in drinking, especially among teenagers, upon the influence of lax newcomers who were undermining the traditional way of life.

The overall impression from the 47 respondents, however, was one of complacency even though many referred to the presence of widespread under age drinking and occasional youthful binge drinking, a situation confirmed by the data collected by the research team on YTS trainees. However, most respondents did not see the binge drinking as a major problem. It was a 'natural' phase that most young people grew out of. Such behaviour took place on only one night a week because of lack of money. Such behaviour might lead to the occasional fist fights but these two communities were law abiding localities with few social problems. Binge drinking may have been tolerated but under age drinking was positively supported by most respondents. It destroyed the association of first time public house entry with the achievement of 'manliness' and adulthood. Young people learned how to operate in that environment in a sensible manner, partly because they were under considerable pressure to conform within their tight knit communities. Unruly behaviour could be fed back by the publican to parents. Early entry to the public house encouraged maturity in the young people and reduced the chances of later alcohol misuse.

Since the completion of the fieldwork, the 'problem' of teenage drinking in Westcross has been highlighted on at least two occasions by the local press. These stories have painted a very different and more disturbing picture of such drinking and the extent to which it encourages crime and vandalism. These stories also suggest that the police, social workers and probation officers are now more concerned about this issue than they were at the time of interview. For example, one story spoke of how:

> "Alcohol addiction among young people in Westcross is so bad that attempts are to be made to set up a non-alcoholic night club to try and draw teenageers away from public houses. The bid for the night club comes at a time when drink related crime in the area has reached an all-time high and is causing concern among probation officers and social workers."

The quotation raises a series of crucial questions. What level of alcohol consumption by young people is deemed to represent 'addiction' by the reporter? Why and how do young people use public houses? How clearcut is the relationship between alcohol consumption and criminal offences? Is the same behaviour by young people being interpreted in different ways by different 'professionals' or is their actual behaviour becoming more problematic? If it is the latter, can and should alcohol be separated out as the only explanation or does it reflect the enthusiasm of the media for shock/horror stories about young people, irrespective of the actual facts? These important questions will be addressed again in the final chapter of this report.

References

1. This issue is discussed in more detail in A. Franklin (1985), Pub drinking and the licensed trade: a study of drinking cultures and local community in two areas of South West England, School for Advanced Urban Studies, University of Bristol, Occasional Paper No 21.

2. For an interesting discussion of these issues see 'Suffer the little children", Free House, (February 1985), pp 6-7.

3. For a discussion of this theory see E. Pitman (1984), Transactional analysis for social workers and counsellors: an introduction, Routledge and Kegan Paul, London.

4. C. Rogers (1951), Client centered therapy, Constable, London.

5. National Marriage Guidance Council (1984), Counsellor basic training prospectus, NMGC, Rugby.

6. DHSS (1981), Care in action - a handbook of policies and priorities for the health and personal social services in England, HMSO, London.

7. The potential of this questionnaire for schools is discussed in J. Balding (1984), 'The use of a general questionnaire on health related behaviour in curriculum planning in secondary schools', pp 113-122 from Health education and youth: a review of research and developments, ed. G. Campbell, Falmer Press, London.

8. The implications of this are discussed in R. Means et al (1985), 'Implementation of social goals in labour market policy: the case of black youth, equal opportunities and the

Youth Training Scheme', Policy and Politics, Vol 13, No 1, pp 71-83.

9. J. Balding (1985), 'The health related behaviour data bank', Education and Health, Vol 3, No 2, pp 29-45.

10. A general discussion of the difficulties of interpreting self reported drinking behaviour can be found in L. Midanik (1982), 'The validity of self reported alcohol consumption and alcohol problems: a literature review', British Journal of Addiction, Vol 77, pp 357-382.

5

ALCOHOL EDUCATION IN ST. ALDHELMS

The locality

St. Aldhelms is a large interwar council estate in the South of a city of nearly 400,000 people. The 1981 census indicates that the two wards that cover the estate have 22,591 residents. The actual estate population would be about 3,000 less.

St. Aldhelms is situated in a city noted for its prosperity and high rates of employment over the last hundred years. From the late 19th century onwards, a small group of firms achieved a pivotal position in the local economy through their ability to cater for the new mass retail market for standard goods at a price affordable by many working class consumers. The interwar years saw the growth of aircraft and munitions industries[1] which received a massive boost from the 1935 rearmament process.

These traditional industries continued to boom in the first 20 years after the war but then overall job losses in manufacturing started to be quite severe. Unemployment rates began to rise in the city to above the national average in the early 1970s although they returned to below the national average later in the decade. This reflected the renewed buoyancy of defence industry generated employment and a rapid growth of service sector employment. The city is now the headquarters of five insurance companies. Registered unemployment at 11.2% in December 1984 was less than the national average.

However, this encouraging overall picture covers up enormous disparities in both the city and its surrounding commuter towns and villages. Companies have been attracted both to the attractive city centre and by the motorway access to the North of the city. There are high rates of unemployment, bad housing and other signs of deprivation in the non-gentrified parts of the inner city and in much of the Southern half of the city. Political and local media interest tends to focus on either the black community in the inner area or the large post war council estates on the fringe of the city. The latter were built with the intention of re-locating a great deal of manufacturing industry to the South with the encouragement of a series of link roads to the motorway. These roads were not built and the firms (with one notable exception) did not arrive.

In January 1983, a development strategy group of chief officers in the city council produced a report on the two main post war council estates, which housed 27,000 people. The report confirmed that many properties were difficult to let; there was a concentration of single parent families; rent arrears were rising; there was a shortage of community facilities, and:

> "although this area is the size of a small town, there are few jobs actually within it and there has been a substantial decline recently in the jobs available in nearby areas. Often jobs can only be found further afield, and the travelling costs can be prohibitive, particularly for lower paid youngsters and unskilled workers. This, coupled with the fact that unemployment in and around the area is increasing alarmingly, is a strong justification for creating and positively promoting new jobs in the area."

Far less attention has been paid to the St. Aldhelms estate and yet it contains many of the same problems.

St. Aldhelms was built in stages during the interwar years under a variety of different Housing Acts. The most important fact about these Acts was that each one was financed by central government in a different way. The early Acts required the local authority to set high rent levels and so tended to attract 'better off' working class families. The later Acts were often restricted to the rehousing of slum clearance families and so rents were set at a lower level. This led to a spread of rent levels on interwar corporation estates that was particularly complex in St. Aldhelms.

A major housing survey was carried out in the city during 1937 and this showed that there was tension between the various groups of residents who had arrived at the estate under the different Acts. In particular, lower middle class families and skilled working class families were attempting to leave St. Aldhelms out of resentment at the arrival of slum clearance families as a result of the later Acts.

133

These slum clearance families had been moved into better quality housing, but they were also living in a locality that was further away from the main job opportunities for unskilled labour. The authors of the 1937 survey warned that:

> "the exceptional poverty on the estate was certainly due in part to the high incidence of unemployment or casual labour. Nearly one quarter of the families on the estate were found to have heads who were either out of work or casually employed."

These unemployed families were provided with few amenities or social services compared with the central districts of the town. The result was physical isolation. The survey authors argued for a positive policy from the local authority in encouraging the development of a community. One mechanism for achieving this would be to allow residents to run the local authority owned social centre and have complete control over its development.

The initial, but perhaps superficial, impression of the research team was that little had changed over the last 50 years. Unemployment is high - St. Aldhelms still contains many of the poorest and most deprived families in the city. A newly formed community association is trying to persuade the local authority to give them control of the same social centre referred to in the 1937 survey. The city council has recently produced an as yet unpublished report on poverty in the city. Local press coverage of this report indicates that it confirms that the Southern half of the city and St. Aldhelms in particular has major problems of deprivation in terms of unemployment, housing conditions and personal resources such as car ownership.

There are few licensed outlets on the St. Aldhelms estate. There is just one public house and one licensed club. There are three public houses on the immediate periphery of the estate. The estate also contains an off licence and a grocery store with a retail licence. Residents, therefore, frequently travel to the city centre or other neighbourhoods when they wish to have a drink in a public house or licensed club.[2]

In this locality study, 52 respondents were contacted and these can be broken down into the categories listed in Table 20. Some of these respondents had responsibilities based on the whole of the city council, the whole of the county council or the whole of the district health authority. The majority of those contacted, however, had a more specific focus on the South of the city and especially the St. Aldhelms council house estate.

Table 20: Discussions held for the St. Aldhelms locality study

Subject area of respondent		No. of repondents
1. Alcohol and specialist provision in the voluntary sector	a) The Council on Alcoholism	2
	b) Self help groups	1
2. Alcohol and the NHS	a) Psychiatric services	2
	b) Health education officers	2
	c) Schools of nursing	5
	d) Primary health care	8
3. Counselling services and alcohol education	a) Statutory agencies	2
	b) Voluntary agencies	2
	c) Churches	1
4. Alcohol and the education department	a) Schools	7
	b) Youth service	7
	c) Colleges of further education	3
5. Alcohol and the law	a) Police	2
	b) Magistrates	1
6. Miscellaneous	a) Youth training scheme	2
	b) Community Programme project	2
	c) Community worker and residents association	3
TOTAL		52

Alcohol and specialist provision in the voluntary sector

(a)   The Council on Alcoholism

The Council on Alcoholism was established in 1969 and initially covered only the city. It extended its boundaries to include the whole county at the time of local government reorganisation of 1974. The present director of the Council has been in post since 1979.

Like the majority of voluntary organisations, the survival of the Council on Alcoholism is dependent upon a complex and not very stable system of finance. Some funding is received from four different district health authorities and from the social services department. All these grants have to be renewed on an annual basis. Additional money is received from a variety of services, including the Manpower Services Commission (MSC), to employ workers to run a library service. Joint finance money has been obtained from health and social services to fund an education officer and the initial finance runs out in August 1986.

The director has to take primary responsibility for maintaining this package and for the supervision and encouragement of the growing number of workers whether paid, seconded or 'volunteers'. There is an office administrator and full time secretary. A nurse used to be seconded full time from one district health authority. This post holder used to offer the main counselling service to problem drinkers. Increasingly, this individual has concentrated upon managing and supporting the growing number of volunteer counsellors (at the time of interview, there were 10 with five more in training). This secondment arrangement has now been ended and the district health authority now provides a grant to cover this post.

The education officer had spent much of his first year doing one-off talks as a result of commitments made in the grant application. The director felt this officer was now in a position to clarify priorities. His responsibilities included the supervision of the MSC funded library staff. There was a projects co-ordinator who looked after a minimal support home which received most of its referrals from the NHS treatment unit. She also supervised an Alcohol Advisory Service (funded until August 1986) in one of the towns in the county which was run by a locally based worker. This worker co-ordinated the work of a further seven volunteer counsellors. Finally, the programme co-ordinator of the HEC's South West alcohol education programme was an employee of the Council on Alcoholism prior to her resignation in April 1985.

In his first two years, the director concentrated upon developing counselling services for problem drinkers. In 1983/84, there were 689 referrals of which 469 were seen. 258 of these were new cases and 211 were known previously. Of the total referrals, 57% were male and 43% were female. These clients generated 2,052 interviews and 1,488 telephone counselling sessions. In the last three years, there has been a greater focus on educational work. The 1983/84 annual report listed 25 types of talk and course provided by staff. These represented a wide range of approaches, including one-off school talks about 'alcoholism' and how it can be tackled. However, this work has also included the development of Drinkwatch courses that draw on materials and are run for teachers, social workers, GPs etc. These were originally developed primarily by the director and a health education officer. This work mushroomed and provided part of the argument for an education officer in the subsequent grant application.

There is a debate within the Council on Alcoholism about the best balance between counselling provision and education provision. The two tasks are seen as fairly separate. There is both a treatment and rehabilitation sub-committee and a prevention and education sub-committee. The director saw this as a positive separation because it reflected an operational split within the organisation. At the same time, there was a competition for resources and those keen on counselling could often be critical of what they saw as 'fancy educational ideas'.

However, the split between counselling and education was less apparent in the director's comments in the 1983/84 annual report. He stressed the need to develop both "educational and counselling services which are accessible to people" and explained that this involved entering "a dialogue with local communities and organisations where we ask them what they think and what they need". His report said there would be forums on alcohol abuse by the end of the year, including one in the South of the city. He explained that "people representing a cross section of the community come to these meetings and we listen to what they say about how services should develop". Several members of the forum in the South of the city were visited and the forum is further considered at the end of this chapter.

The education officer stressed the depth and diversity of his present educational activities. As well as the one-off sessions clearly referred to, he had run two Drinking choices courses - one for the youth service and one for the probation service. He was involved in the training of voluntary counsellors for the Council on Alcoholism. He was responsible for the supervision of the Alcohol Library and Information Service, and this was increasingly developing an outreach function in which MSC funded workers visited agencies and groups to discuss their information needs. He had helped to run two short courses in <u>Introducing drugs and drug use</u> for council members and others in the past year. These events had been jointly run with the South West Regional Drug Training Unit. He was involved in discussions with the education authority and teachers about the alcohol education needs of schools.

Overall, he felt that his activities had concentrated on the 'secondary prevention' end of education rather than 'primary prevention' but he hoped to be able to become more involved in public education-type activities in the future. He felt alcohol educators should not establish priority groups before they have been involved in a dialogue with neighbourhood based groups. The education officer expressed frustration that his work tended to become defined as running courses for professionals. He would prefer to foster a community development approach that encouraged a debate about alcohol at the local level. The forums on alcohol abuse were failing to maintain the interest of community representatives. Local groups needed to be encouraged to develop policies and to exert influence on local licensing and advertising decisions. They should question the paucity of expenditure by local authorities and health authorities on health and alcohol education relative to the costs of treatment.

(b)   Self help groups

Alcoholics Anonymous has a main office in the city which covers an area with 70 or more AA groups. Referrals are made from a wide range of agencies including GPs, psychiatric and general hospitals, the Council on Alcoholism and private treatment units. The AA fellowship has a particularly good relationship with the local NHS treatment unit.

Some members of AA carry out counselling as part of their professional roles and the London office has recently produced guidelines for those carrying out this function. Locally, members attend the Council on Alcoholism to train as counsellors.

The fellowship had responded positively to the HEC alcohol education programme and the representative contacted was enthusiastic about the part education could play in preventing individuals from becoming alcoholics. He felt that the education authorities should ensure that alcohol education takes place both in primary and secondary schools.

Alcohol and the NHS

(a) Psychiatric services

The main treatment unit for the city operates as a 20 place day hospital and is run by the district health authority that covers the South of the city. It was originally intended as a 25 place in-patient unit, but the finance for this was never provided. The consultant explained that in-patients had to be kept at two psychiatric hospitals.

If the unit was larger, the consultant would encourage earlier referral. He had one hospital referral in which a patient had been admitted 10 times before liver cirrhosis was officially diagnosed. However, he could not cope with a greater volume of referrals and so it was pointless to seek them. If he did, 'disposal' became his problem. In any case, other physicians were often reluctant to part with patients that have alcohol related diseases.

The consultant explained that patients at the unit were not allowed to drink; this reflected how far they were down the alcoholic road. One year after the treatment there was a 60% improvement rate. In other words, six had not touched alcohol for 12 months; two would have died from drink; two would still be struggling. He suspected staff sometimes lost morale because they only saw the failures, ie those who kept coming back.

Controlled drinking offered a way forward for some problem drinkers but not all. It was particularly relevant for those who drank heavily under peer group pressure. However, abstinence was a necessity for those who regularly misused alcohol to cover up psychological problems associated with personal inadequacy. The strength of AA is that it offers a self help group in which abstaining alcoholics can understand and cope with these underlying weaknesses and problems.[3] Abstinence was required for those with a physiological dependence since controlled drinking could not save a damaged liver.

A massive increase in alcohol education was necessary, especially with young people from primary school onwards. There needed to be a greater realisation of how easily alcohol could become a problem for the individual. There were now one million problem drinkers in this country. However, this did not lead him to favour a temperance approach. Methodists and Mormons had negative attitudes to alcohol, yet suffered high rates of alcoholism. Jewish families had a healthy, positive attitude and there were far less difficulties.

A meeting was also held with a community psychiatric nurse who worked from the main psychiatric hospital of the district health authority that covers St. Aldhelms. He received referrals from hospital consultants but he was also linked to several GPs in the South of the city, including those in the health centre in the middle of the St. Aldhelms estate. He has developed a specialist interest in solvent abuse and was mentioned in this connection by several of the other respondents. He said that the South of the city had a massive drug problem, but few people with the interest or skill to tackle it. It was easy to exaggerate numbers in areas such as solvent abuse, but it did affect a sizeable minority. These tended to be low achievers with no self confidence and often little parental support. 'Hobby kids' and 'doers' did not abuse solvents on a regular basis. Solvent abusers do risk brain damage from sniffing. However, he believed the habit was now far less common or popular, although it did now attract children as young as nine or ten. Most adolescents have moved on to 'alcohol, pills and powders'. Binge drinking was common and heroin was very cheap. He felt pessimistic about the future.

He thought the central blame for this situation had to be put on the general environment of the estate and the lack of job prospects. Many youngsters on the estate were pessimistic about their chances of obtaining work after school, and these feelings developed very early, often through their awareness of what was happening to older siblings. The estate had few community facilities that could direct energy in a more creative way. These problems had to be tackled if the overall problem of drug abuse on council estates was to be reduced. Involving local youngsters in the creation and control of such facilities was essential.

(b)   Health education officers

One health education officer was visited before the planned devolution of HEOs from a central area health clinic to district health authorities had taken place. This officer had responsibilities for a variety of health topics, including mental health, heart and stroke, cancer, back pain and sight. She was also responsible for health education in the area of drugs and alcohol where the bulk of work tended to be on smoking.

However, her interest in alcohol education was very strong. In the mid seventies, she joined the Executive Committee of the Council on Alcoholism, but found that her health education initiatives met with massive resistance in the NHS. Assumptions were made that the aim was to prohibit drinking. It was believed the problem concerned only a few weak willed people who drifted down a slippery slope into alcoholism. There was embarrassment at the volume of drink consumed at NHS social functions. This officer abandoned her efforts to develop this type of work until she started to receive support from the new director of the Council on Alcoholism. In 1982, she obtained a copy of the Drinking choices manual at a course in York. This resulted in one of the authors being asked to run a one day conference for a multi-disciplinary group of teachers, probation officers, youth workers and NHS staff. From this, a Drinking choices planning group was formed, and a variety of courses run. A major Drinkwatch campaign was carried out on drink and driving in which 88 GPs in the county agreed to display leaflets. She was convenor of one of the alcohol abuse forums.

This officer in all her areas of responsibility placed a heavy emphasis upon school liaison. She attends the Primary School Heads Committee and the Secondary Heads Committee meetings. She believed that most schools in the county made heavy use of the Loan/Resource Unit of the central area health clinic and this was supported by the researchers' discussions with teachers and school nurses.

The second HEO was seen after the reorganisation of the central unit into district health authorities and she worked for the authority that covered St. Aldhelms. The role and priorities of the new department were still in the process of being decided. This involved assessing the views of the various health professionals about priorities and possible strategies; it also involved making decisions about what activities to maintain from the work of HEOs in the previous unit. In this situation, alcohol education had no automatic right to priority although she was impressed by the previous work of the HEO referred to above, and did accept that there was a wide range of health problems created by alcohol.

The HEO felt health education needed to be eclectic in its approach. Sometimes the behaviour of individuals needed to be changed (eg uptake of vaccination) but this was an exception and not the rule. More often she preferred people to make their own choices, but this could involve helping people to convert decisions into actions. Sometimes a social change model was required; this did not focus on individuals or small groups but rather on changing the environment (eg making non alcoholic drinks more acceptable).

More specifically with regard to alcohol, she thought people ought to realise that drink was often being used as a means of escape from other problems. Why alcohol was chosen rather than another crutch was due to cultural factors. These involved norms about how much to drink, the availability of drink etc. One factor that might be significant was the availability and cost of alcohol since these would influence what was chosen as an appropriate crutch, but this was only part of the picture. If alcohol did become less available, then people might turn to something else. Reducing availability might be treating the symptoms rather than the cause of the problems.

(c)   Schools of nursing

Discussions were held with five nurse tutors from the same district health authority. Information was also collected on in-service training. The nurse tutors drew attention to the recent interest taken by the nursing profession in the issue of stress and the influence this may have on heavy drinking. The National Staff Committee had produced a booklet for managers on how to recognise and give assistance with alcohol problems. This concern was reflected to some extent in the in-service training provided within the health district for nurses and nurse managers. The head of in-service training was unfortunately on sick leave but it was possible to clarify that a two day alcohol study course was provided for nurse managers. This was designed to alert managers to the impact of alcoholism on nurses. The course included outside speakers from AA and the Council on Alcoholism as well as people from the out-patient treatment unit. It covered issues such as factors which contribute to alcoholism, facts about alcohol and attitudes towards it, and the disciplinary process.

The main alcohol related input into nurse training was given to psychiatric nurse students who had to spend up to 12 weeks at the out-patient treatment unit as part of a module on alcoholism and addiction. Other nurses received a much more varied input, although in general it was not an area that received a high priority or generated great interest. For example, lectures on alcoholism within the hospital were made open to nursing staff but very few attended.

The nurse tutors felt hospital patients were not blamed for their alcohol related problems but were seen as not being able to help themselves. The medical model was used only for acute cases who needed drying out. Other cases were referred to the helping agencies. At the same time frustration was sometimes felt towards repeat admissions while accident/emergency units did not always offer an effective response. One reason for the inadequate response was the lack of a standard procedure for dealing with alcohol problems, which was compounded by the fact that junior doctors tended to have little training for dealing with social problems. Doctors would often send the patient back home, while nursing staff would be more likely to refer to a social worker.

The tutors' views on alcohol education were less clearly defined. They felt most people were rational about drinking and only a small minority faced problems. At the same time, they complained about both the general advertising pressure to increase social drinking and the tendency for health professionals to define drug addiction and alcohol misuse as self induced personal problems. Like the second HEO mentioned above, they emphasised that stress, whether from pressure of work or the lack of it, was the major factor in alcohol misuse. They also felt that GPs were poorly trained to pick up alcohol related problems in patients who did not define this as the immediate problem.

(d)   Primary health care

Seven health visitors were seen while less successful attempts were made to see local GPs. They were based on two health centres; one of them was in the middle of the St. Aldhelms estate and the second on the periphery.

There was general agreement that residents on the estate were not 'health conscious' in terms of diet, smoking or the consumption of other drugs, and that this needed to be understood in relation to poverty and bad housing on the estate rather than the pathological inadequacy of residents.

Views were much more varied about the nature of drinking patterns and drinking problems on the estate. One health visitor pointed out that she has little contact with male residents and she knew of only one who was having difficulties in child care through drink. She felt there was no tradition of female drinking on the estate, and drink problems stood out in her caseload because of their infrequency. The health centre held a lunchtime Christmas party for mums. Sherry was provided but only drunk by the staff. Most families do not have drink in the house. Stress from poor housing, debt and marital conflict was, therefore, more likely to be responded to with a high demand for tranquillisers. Many families on the estate were composed of three generations. Young mothers were often well supported; the middle class mothers with young children who drank at home out of depression and isolation did not have many working class equivalents on the estate. Her colleague, on the other hand, stressed her concern at how her caseload of elderly clients included growing numbers of drinkers who were attempting to cope with various forms of loss and bereavement with alcohol.

The health visitors in the other health centre also stressed that drinking by men was far more prevalent than drinking by women. In fact their main contact with alcohol was through individuals in families who had developed social problems associated with drinking. These were usually not health problems, but marital violence or lack of resources due to money being spent on drink. They rarely interviewed anyone who was in an alcoholic state, although this might be because most of their visits were pre-planned. They felt that in a poor working class area, drink problems became apparent before people had become dependent, and that this contrasted with middle class areas.

They felt that people drank because they were bored, lonely or depressed and it was their way of giving themselves 'a treat'; it was a form of comfort. They felt there was little they could do for people who were not actually alcoholic. People who were well motivated would seek out counselling help from agencies such as the Marriage Guidance Council. It also seemed ridiculous suggesting to young women with three children that they should give up drinking and smoking. What other pleasures did they have?

They were enthusiastic about the need for an expansion in alcohol education. The general public was very badly informed about the alcoholic content of drinks and the amount women could drink before damaging their health.

Both groups of health visitors felt GPs tended to be poor health educators. Numerous attempts were made to meet with at least two GPs from the health centre in the middle of the estate. The medical secretary was telephoned and letters were sent. Eventually a telephone message was received indicating that the doctors 'were not interested'.

Counselling services and alcohol education

(a) Statutory agencies

Two social workers were contacted. One of these was a middle manager in an office that covered an adjacent council estate to St. Aldhelms. The other was a field worker in the social work team that covered much of St. Aldhelms. The second of these was one of the names most frequently mentioned to the research team in connection with alcohol education in the area. He has carried out a research dissertation on alcohol related problems in social work cases which replicated a previous Lothian study.[4]   One in five family cases (ie 42) with one or more children under 18 were found to have such problems in the district studied.   This social worker has since persuaded the social services department to support the establishment of an alcohol advice centre in another area in the South of the city.   He was also a member of the Council on Alcoholism and an instigator of the alcohol abuse forum that covered all the communities in this part of the city.   The alcohol advice centre was a joint project between the social services department and the Council on Alcoholism.   Staff and premises were provided by the social services department; it was open on Thursday afternoons.   In the first six months, 30 referrals were received and 21 clients seen.   A large number of educational activities were also carried out.

In general, this social worker believed his colleagues lacked either the confidence to address drinking issues with their clients or the skill to pick up drinking clues.   This was seen as a serious failing for reasons outlined in his dissertation:

> "Evidence from this and the Lothian study suggests that alcohol related problems are embedded within general problems found in day-to-day family case-work. Relationship difficulties were ascertained as crucial areas of family disfunction.   Many of these cases are multi-problematical, take up much time, effort and commitment, involve statutory duties, tend to be of long duration and seem not to be destined for specialist referral.   Specifically, large numbers of children known to this department as a result of neglect and abuse, care, supervision and matrimonial orders, may be facing alcohol related problems within their family network. Alcohol abuse is a threat to family stability which adds to a range of risks and stresses that the family unit

faces today. An increased understanding of the effects on children is needed by social workers, and also by those involved in residential day care and home care services."

Several of the clients of the alcohol advice centre came from the St. Aldhelms estate. However, this social worker was not keen to reflect on drinking patterns on the estate. Probation officers and social workers have a drink on getting home from work. Businessmen drink at lunchtime. The often poor residents of St. Aldhelms had their own patterns of alcohol consumption. Different groups drink in different ways. It was a national problem fed by 'macho' image advertising.

This social worker expressed enthusiasm for more alcohol education. There was a need to focus on issues that grasped attention such as alcohol and crime, and alcohol and workplace accidents. Alcohol and drug education needed to be an integral part of the curricula of all schools. At the same time, he expressed concern that an emphasis on education could be used to justify a resource reduction for treatment services. He said he was unsure about how Councils on Alcoholism should respond in terms of establishing a balance between treatment and education.

The second social worker supervised the previous respondent's work at the alcohol advice centre. He was chair of the local alcohol abuse forum, a member of the treatment sub-committee of the Council on Alcoholism, and he had been on a Key Tutor course. He felt that many social workers did not address the problem of drink with their clients, even though it might be leading to violence and debt. They would discuss crime, sex or any other personal problem yet discussion of drinking behaviour was seen as taboo and intrusive. He believed there were a number of reasons for this. Alcohol counselling and alcohol education rarely appeared in training courses or in-service training events. Many social workers refused to accept that heavy drinking may be a problem for their clients. Others may lack confidence in their own drinking behaviour.

His primary aim was to develop the capacity of social workers to recognise and then counsel problem drinkers. However, the Drinking choices material and the small sample of school material that he had seen did not seem to place enough emphasis upon an alcohol free life-style as a viable alternative to the sensible drinking model.

146

(b)   Voluntary agencies

The director of the Samaritans in the city said they did deal with a steady flow of problem drinkers, most of whom were older people. These cases were usually referred to AA. If they have someone in distress from drink, AA will come to the office or to the client's home whatever the time. More limited use was also made of Al Anon, the out-patient treatment unit and the Council on Alcoholism. The director suspected drink related problems were growing, especially from increased consumption by women and young people. This was not yet being reflected in the Samaritans' workload. They were not often approached by young people. There was a general tendency for people to show reluctance in accepting that they have a drink problem. The Samaritans have a rule that they will not see someone when he/she is actually drunk. They feel they need professional help in handling people with drink and drug problems. The organiser of the Marriage Guidance Council gave a similar set of responses. The same agencies are used for the referral of problem drinkers and general satisfaction was expressed about these services. The organiser had been counselling for 12 years and felt that drink was now mentioned as a problem more often than it used to be. One reason for this was that the public house was one of the few places where couples on average or below average incomes could afford to go together.

(c)   The churches

One church official was seen, a Roman Catholic priest whose church was in the centre of St. Aldhelms. His point of view was similar to that of the health visitors. The bulk of pastoral problems brought to him by parishioners concerned family problems such as conflict between husband and wife, and between parents and adolescent children. However, these tensions and conflicts were often magnified by the poverty and deprivation of the estate. This poverty and deprivation was a reflection not only of bad housing and unemployment but also of the housing allocation policies of the council. The whole estate represented a narrow social band and parts of it were used to house 'multi problem families' such as those with high rent arrears, single parents or those suffering from various forms of mental disability.

As a result, many parts of the estate had few resources and experienced poor educational opportunities. Half the pupils in the Roman Catholic primary school had special educational needs. Health care was appalling. Low income, poor education, bad housing, unemployment and social and psychological stress all

147

created a situation in which health education could not thrive. He felt people lived on a survival level. People bought expensive food from the local corner shop because they lacked the self confidence to shop further afield.

He argued that drinking patterns needed to be understood in relation to the above situation. He said that alcohol was an important part of life on the estate for many people, but that drinking outlets were very limited. Three types of drinking pattern caused him most concern. First, alcohol was being severely abused by a group of middle aged cider drinkers who sat out at the main shopping street on the estate. Second, there was the club or pub drinker who felt a need to go every night as an escape from the home. Third, there was the process of taking drink home from the off licence so that it can be used as an anaesthetic. He did not see every visit to an off licence or a pub as a problem and he did not want to condemn local people for excessive drinking. People drank because of stress, and yet drink could cause more stress through its cost or its capacity to cause physical dependence. He saw solvent abuse as being generated from the same stress and feelings of alienation. Glue was also an anaesthetic but one lacking general social acceptability; this increased the attractiveness of glue for many youngsters on the estate.

The priest felt that this situation meant there was a major need for health education and alcohol education on the estate. However, he felt such activities would be very difficult to launch effectively or constructively. It would easily be seen as "them getting at us again", and so any campaign could easily feed into what he called the "corporate inferiority complex of the estate". The isolation of alcohol from the broader problem of deprivation on the estate might put further blame on people for their own problems. Alcohol education initiatives in St. Aldhelms would have to show a clear recognition of the magnitude of the housing and unemployment issues on the estate and should be carried out through existing groups that aleady had some level of acceptance.

Alcohol and young people

(a)   Schools

The adviser for pastoral and social education emphasised that the county had a long tradition of interest in health education. From the early seventies the county was used by the Schools Council to experiment in health education curricula for five to 13 year olds and then for 13 to 18 year olds. The county was chosen by Her Majesty's Inspectorate to illustrate good practice in a report on health education.

She believed health education should be integrated into a broad range of personal and social activities in schools. It should not be seen as esoteric and separate, although discrete content areas such as sex education needed to be addressed. Such an approach required an emphasis upon group work and participative learning. The adviser believed that in many respects the method (ie participative learning) was more important than the content. She felt teachers found it difficult to accept this kind of approach because it was not reflected in their training. This meant teachers needed considerable support and in-service training. All schools have been encouraged to carry out curricula reviews so that concepts of personal development can be integrated throughout.

With regard to alcohol education, the adviser felt that delicate and sensitive issues should emerge as naturally as possible through a focus on life processes. Issues such as alcohol, drugs and sex should emerge as topics from an overall concern with decision making and choice. At the same time, she was aware and concerned that many young people were becoming more self destructive. Because of this, she was becoming less certain about her antagonism to a shock/horror approach. However, it should still be used only if it was grafted on to an overall preventive approach where the emphasis was on encouraging young people to make and understand their own choices.

Staff from three schools were visited, namely two head teachers, three other teachers and a school nurse. All of these schools served or partially served the St. Aldhelms estate. In one school, the social education co-ordinator and a group of other staff had reviewed the social education syllabus two years ago. Every pupil now received one social education lesson per week. Previously, this kind of lesson had only been available to the 'less able' but it was felt this meant that the 'more able' were missing out. The new syllabus has one general aim and seven underlying objectives. The aim was "to develop pupils' knowledge and understanding of society and their present and future roles within it". The seven objectives included "to create a positive attitude towards leisure activities". In the first year, the emphasis was on enabling pupils to settle down and feel confident at a secondary school. In the second year, information was given on a variety of topics, but with a heavy focus on smoking. Possible careers were the main focus of the third year, while the fourth year syllabus looked at teenage development and the pressures/influences upon emerging lifestyles. The final year returned to the focus on careers work. Alcohol education was addressed in the fourth year under Abuses of health together with obesity, glue sniffing and anorexia. Teachers were allocated to such topics on the basis of both interest and availability. As a result, different approaches might be taken by different teachers. Some were interested in the underlying objectives while others were only concerned with the content of particular lessons. Some favoured a more shock/horror approach than others. Some teachers refused to take alcohol education seriously. A further problem was that the careers input of the fifth year was now being started in the fourth year because it was seen as so essential; the time available to address health education issues was therefore being squeezed.

The other two schools were operating social education curricula that had not been reviewed recently, and teachers at both schools expressed some dissatisfaction with present arrangements. Health education was tackled in one school during the fourth and fifth years as part of a module on community education. The 'more able' were not expected to take this. The health education sessions looked at health issues such as smoking, sexual diseases and alcoholism. Under alcoholism, pupils were told about what happens when you drink, alcohol and the law, and the helping organisations. Speakers were invited from AA and the Council on Alcoholism. In the third year, human biology looked at the impact of alcohol on the body although the social education co-ordinator had only just discovered this was happening. Tutor group studies might also raise this kind of subject. For example, pupils invited outsiders to a Christmas party and this was used to discuss how alcohol is used at such events. In the final school, the main input on alcohol education came from a biology teacher where one element of his course in the third year dealt with alcohol, drugs and glue sniffing. The emphasis of these lessons was on providing facts about the harm that alcohol does to the body. Alcohol was addressed in less detail in the fourth and fifth year when all pupils took a social education stream. This situation had been reviewed recently because it was felt that the health education element of social education was poorly developed, and that the biology syllabus was being squeezed by the present emphasis on health education issues. The review failed to produce changes for two reasons. First, there was conflict among staff about the value of a more formal health education input into social education: some preferred to develop and address such issues in more informal ways in tutor groups.

Second, the school was scheduled to close because of falling rolls and this made it difficult to interest staff in curricula change. However, this school was running an in-service training day in July 1985 on drug, solvent and alcohol abuse.

Staff at the three schools mentioned certain difficulties in attempting innovation in the area of health education. One was the general uncertainty about schooling arrangements in the South of the city; councillors from different political parties were agreed about the problem of falling rolls but there was no consensus about how best to respond to this. Second, staff morale was further lowered by anger at the failure of pay negotiations. Third, some teachers felt health education and social education issues squeezed the 'normal' syllabus and reduced the chances of the 'more able' to pass exams.

All the teachers were asked about their perceptions of attitudes to drink among pupils and parents. The question of under age drinking is a sensitive one in schools and very mixed replies were received. These replies also reflected the attitude of staff to drink. One teacher had a very hostile attitude to drink and, therefore, any teenage drinking caused her great anxiety. There seemed to be a wide agreement, however, that St. Aldhelms residents had a very ready acceptance of drink and that this was passed on to teenagers. Two teachers expressed concern at the amount of alcohol kept in the home. Young people were seen as being 'at risk' from alcohol abuse and solvent abuse, but that parents were only concerned about the latter. One head teacher stressed that glue attracts the loners and alcohol the socialisers. Another respondent stressed that the same sizeable minority with a personality weakness was tempted to misuse both drugs; mixing cider drinking and glue sniffing was becoming more common. Many felt poor job prospects encouraged self destructive behaviour in young people.

(b)   The youth.service[5]

Seven staff from the youth service were interviewed. One of these repondents was a middle manager based in the city centre. He stressed that under age drinking was not seen as a problem so long as the alcohol was not consumed on youth club premises. There was often an attitude of keeping the troublemakers out. This complacency was undermined by the 1980 'moral panic' about solvent abuse. He said that many youth workers felt the growth of solvent abuse was linked to the recession. Some of them expressed concern that the recession was also encouraging excessive drinking at an earlier age. This youth officer had had a long interest in alcohol education and he was able to persuade these workers to go on a <u>Drinking choices</u> course run by the health education officer whose work was reviewed earlier in this chapter. The course encountered difficulties. Some participants felt the course was run in too didactic a manner. Others refused to discuss their own drinking behaviour as they considered it irrelevant. The course had not been followed up, partly because there was no training officer within the service. The officer felt drink and drug problems were worsening in most parts of the city. Opportunities for young people were declining because of lack of work, lack of interesting work and lack of excitement especially in villages and some council estates. Different tensions existed in high income areas. Middle class parents were getting more and more anxious about the employment prospects for their children. Enormous pressure was placed on children to be academically successful.

A more detailed view of how solvent abuse and alcohol abuse may interconnect was offered by three staff with detailed knowledge of the large post war council estates in the South of the city. The first of these emphasised that he dealt with those young people who were most 'at risk'. He said drinking and solvent abuse became frequent in boys and girls from 13 years onwards. They sniff glue and then drink cider and lager. Young people get into this pattern of behaviour for two main reasons. First, they may want to forget; in these situations drug consumption often led to depression. Second, they may want confidence; drug consumption then often led to fighting. The cost of drink and drugs encouraged stealing by the time young people were 16 or 17. The older glue sniffers were beginning to move to heroin. This youth worker was not optimistic about the future. High unemployment and the isolation of the estate encouraged such patterns of behaviour. Glue and cider were cheap and provided escape and a route to excitement. Few alternatives could be offered that were within the financial resources of residents.

This pattern of behaviour was confirmed by one of his colleagues. He stressed that young people on the estate had little disposable income. They were able to consume by stealing goods or stealing money to buy the goods. Alcohol was stolen from local supermarkets. Under age drinking was also common. He said that in Liverpool, Newcastle and Manchester there was a strong culture of heavy drinking but under age drinking was more controlled by publicans. Residents in such areas might be short of money, but some was reserved for drinking. The publican still made a living.

152

In St. Aldhelms and the post war council estates, however, the pub trade was badly hit by the recession. The landlords panicked and encouraged mass under age drinking. However, it had taken this officer a long time to perceive alcohol and young people as a problem area. As a student, he believed 'getting pissed' was a part of growing up and heavy drinking was widely accepted and pursued within the youth service. The impact of the recession challenged such views. Unemployed men were taking 13 year old girls to pubs. Weekend binge drinking by 14 and 15 year olds was leading to violence and the regular need for emergency stomach pumping. Young people were starting to mix glue and the cheaper forms of alcohol.

They felt that schools needed to tackle such issues in a more effective way than was happening at present. Schools were afraid that they were losing control of young people. They were not addressing the underlying problems facing young people in this part of the city, such as unemployment. Topics such as glue, alcohol and sex education needed to be linked with these problems and not treated as separate problems addressed in one-off talks by outside experts.

A youth worker based at a youth centre in an adjacent area to St. Aldhelms had a slightly different perspective. He worked with an older age group (17+) who were interested in pursuing high quality sports activities. Heavy drinking (defined as about eight pints a session) was quite common among young males from that area. He did not feel patterns of drinking had changed greatly in recent years. Rather, he wished to emphasise the positive role of the pub in his work with young people, especially if they were unemployed. Team activities at his centre reduced their isolation. However, this was also helped by such groups going to a public house afterwards. The pub has the right relaxed atmosphere. The group will allow the unemployed to boast and express themselves when in the pub. The youth worker was able to talk to unemployed members about their day-to-day pressures. He was thus able to work with the unemployed without having a formal unemployment group which might stigmatise members.

He did not feel that the youth service had a clear policy on educating young people about drug abuse. Training events and materials were generated from the initiative of individuals. The most appropriate approach was a social skills emphasis which encouraged young people to take responsibility for their own behaviour. However, the youth service was inclined to be paternalistic and so suitable materials were often not generated.

The final two respondents had a more direct involvement with service provision in St. Aldhelms. One was a middle manager who supervised several young workers from the South of the city and the other was the leader of a St. Aldhelms youth club. The first of these two stressed that heavy drinking was frequent among 17+ males on the St. Aldhelms estate and that under age drinking was quite common. Residents just did not believe that drinking six or seven pints a night was a health issue, and this made it difficult to address the problem. However, this problem should not be exaggerated. Local youth clubs found it relatively easy to control, although drinking before arrival at a disco was quite common. He agreed it was difficult to know if club users were representative of the local population. The style of the youth worker would influence the clientele. Some attract only safe youngsters; others attract only the difficult ones. He felt youth workers should try to achieve a balance. He did not believe youth provision was intended only for young people with personal difficulties.

The final youth worker ran a youth club on the St. Aldhelms estate for both boys and girls. The official range is 11-21 but most users tended to be between 13 and 16. About 50 people used the centre per night. The club was also open four mornings per week as a day centre for the unemployed. Older males were more loosely associated with the youth centre through various football teams. Drink did crop up as a discipline problem but not very often (ie once every two months). Boys and girls sometimes drank cider in the toilets and they would then become upset or aggressive. It was no more common than it was when he first arrived five years ago; the only difference was that cider drinking was now sometimes linked to glue. The older users go to a local pub after football; the landlord was happy with their behaviour and he did not see them as troublemakers. Local people do drink quite heavily. Six pints is not seen as a heavy session. It was quite a normal pattern of drinking at the social club formed for friends of the youth club. However, this acceptance of heavy drinking did not mean there was any acceptance of anti-social behaviour resulting from drink. This was frowned on regardless of whether it came from adult men or teenage boys. He stressed that his club was used by people from a relatively small number of streets. Residents in this part of St. Aldhelms saw themselves as more 'respectable' than residents in other parts. Complaints from other professionals about mushrooming of drug and alcohol abuse might reflect the fact that they worked on other parts of the estate. He had a general worry that campaigns such as the one on solvent abuse triggered the behaviour it tried to stop. He preferred to counsel young people or groups of young people when they raised the subject themselves.

(c)   Colleges of further education

Three lecturers from the college of further education, whose catchment area included St. Aldhelms, were contacted. The head of liberal studies was responsible for a department which taught the general and communication studies element of City and Guilds courses. This could take up to 16% of the course time. The syllabus was based on the desire to teach certain underlying skills (eg how to process information, how to present information etc) rather than on the importance of certain content areas. The students were offered a 'menu' of topics, but only a small number of them could be followed. A skill based syllabus meant the same syllabus could be applied to students from a wide range of jobs. It was also an attempt to retain the commitment of employers to general and communications studies. This element was in constant danger of being squeezed.

Alcohol education did appear on the 'menu' usually in the guise of drink and driving/riding. The lecturer was very aware of the dangers of this combination through the death of a student over ten years ago. However, this topic was not particularly popular with the students. Most of his students were heavy drinkers, especially if they were day-release engineers; the drinking remained controlled and rarely led into anti-social behaviour. For most, such drinking was considerably reduced as family and domestic commitments increased.

The other two lecturers spent a relatively small percentage of their time working as welfare counsellors for the 1,000 full time and 3,000 part time students. The main problems brought to them were financial, but family tensions, academic worries and drug problems were also common. Alcohol was raised as an issue on only a limited number of occasions. It tended to be raised in one of three forms. The end of term binge might lead to conflict with a landlord and landlady after a drinker returned to his digs; the student usually apologised and all was forgiven. Second, students often complained about the behaviour of parents and sometimes this revolved around the heavy drinking of the father. Third, heavy regular drinking by a student might be a problem but this was very rare; it had mainly occurred on a TOPS preparatory course which is funded by the MSC.

The general student population varied in its interest in drink and local pubs. The nearest pub did market itself for teenage custom and under age drinking did take place. However, money was limited and pubs were used as a warm meeting place as much as for the drink. One counsellor was very critical of the 18 year old rule which he felt made entry to a pub a sign of adulthood; this stimulated a culture of violence and aggression around some teenage drinking that was not found in European countries with more liberal licensing laws. Both stressed that students at the college are treated as mature adults and not pupils; a prescriptive approach to alcohol education would be totally rejected by the students.

Alcohol and the law

(a)   The police

Two officers from the Community Involvement Unit of the relevant division of the police authority were visited. The inspector in charge of this unit was a member of the local alcohol abuse forum and is known for his specialist interest in the area of solvent abuse. The unit was established as part of the Scarman Report[6]-led debate about how to pre-empt the development of future disturbances of the kind that had happened in Brixton and Toxteth in 1981. Much of the work of the unit involved providing speakers for a large number of groups. It involved persuading beat officers to perform this kind of function and to appreciate the need for community liaison. School liaison was a central part of the work. The unit had been instrumental in establishing the Community Programme Project discussed in the next section.

Neither officer expressed a great deal of concern about drinking patterns within their division. There were not many pubs on the estate and many people travelled to adjacent areas for their drinking sessions. Under age drinking required careful watching and some off licences would try to sell drink to anyone. However, they were much more anxious about the solvent abuse situation. Children were now experimenting with glue from six onwards; they picked up glue bags dropped by older children. Fourteen was the peak age for glue sniffing. Those slightly older were mixing glue with cider. However, such behaviour was less of a problem in St. Aldhelms than in some other council estates. He believed that up to 80% of young people in the South of the city would try glue at some stage although only a small minority would become regular users. This minority would tend to be children with other problems such as conflict with parents, unhappiness at school etc.

The full danger of solvents was not appreciated. The inspector was very critical of the 'do it safely' approach to avoiding fatalities. The material distributed to schools by some health education officers was out of date and misleading. Glue damaged the brain. It speeded up the heart rate and could cause heart attacks. Young people would only be persuaded of the dangers if they were given lectures in school by experts who gripped their attention by warning of the likely physical harm.

They felt the reason for this growth of solvent abuse had to be linked to the social and economic position of young people in the main council estates. There was no work, no industry and no community facilities. His school visits underlined the level of apathy even of 14 year olds; they believed their future was made up of YTS and then the dole. Boredom, crime, drug abuse and unemployment were all inter-related. Glue was cheap and reduced boredom. Alternative outlets needed to be created for young people. Young people could not afford to leave the estate and yet there was nothing for them to do there. Thefts and car related offences in St. Aldhelms were massive. On a Sunday morning, the estate was littered with cars stolen from town by those wanting to get back home.

Table 21 indicates the limited statistics they were able to provide on alcohol related offences within their division.

Table 21:   Alcohol related offences in the 'South' division of the police authority

Year	Excess alcohol when breathalysed	Refuse breath test	Drunk	Drunk/ disorderly
1982	144	25	27	12
1983	220	34	29	18
1984	260	38	31	21

(b)   Magistrates

The chairman of the bench for the City's Magistrates' Court felt that alcohol was too frequently used as a defence in offences, irrespective of whether intent has to be shown. His own impression, not based on any statistical evidence, was that more people were coming before him with drink related problems. The probation service, working with the Alcohol Advisory Centre, does provide support, particularly for younger offenders, who are willing to accept an order specifying attendance at alcohol education sessions.

The chairman was not on the licensing committee but was aware of a clamp down on the number of special licences being granted to some pubs. His local police liaison committee, which did not cover the locality study area, had expressed concern over drink in schools and the control of the sale of liquor to young people, particularly from supermarkets. He would be happy to see a ban on all drinking and driving but recognised that public opinion must be changed before this kind of legislation can be enacted.

Miscellaneous

(a)   The Youth Training Scheme

As explained in Chapter Four, youth training schemes are split into two modes of delivery, namely Mode 'A' and Mode 'B'. The latter tended to be characterised as being for 'disadvantaged' young people who were not ready for the world of work. The main social centre on the St. Aldhelms estate houses part of a YTS Mode 'B' scheme. The supervisor for this unit explained there were six female trainees, all from "the bottom end of the market" which she defined as being educationally sub-normal (ESN), disturbed, etc. The unit was part of the overall Mode 'B' provision supplied by a larger training agency. The activities of the unit were focused on providing out of school activities for children under 14 years of age.

The social skills element was very unstructured in the unit. The supervisor encouraged open discussion and the overall aim was to enable young people to learn how to make their own decisions. An open discussion approach was possible because of the small size of the unit. For example, money management was discussed when someone complained of being 'skint'. Topics such as sex and religion were all discussed whenever this was appropriate. Lifestyle issues around the area of drink and drugs, however, were rarely raised by the trainees. The girls in her unit did not go regularly to local public houses or discos; they lacked money to pay for leisure and they lacked confidence in coping with male sexual aggression.

Instead they did babysitting. They listened to records in each other's homes.

The supervisor stressed how the recession had hit St. Aldhelms but that residents would not be helped by "throwing money at them". Many residents had pathological tendencies; they rejected all outsiders and they had a 'ghetto' mentality. This made it difficult to employ them. Parents showed little interest in their children. Women were more likely to be at work than the men. Residents, especially the young, needed to be taught new attitudes and skills. This did not mean being soft and giving in to unreasonable or self destructive behaviour. Professionals tended to do this. She preferred "a fortnight of hell and a lifetime of peace". Young people needed guidelines and rules.

The head of the YTS training unit, which was part of the college of further education, explained that his unit was responsible for all aspects of a 45 place community care scheme and 35 place office skills course. They also offered up to 13 weeks' 'off the job' training for a variety of other schemes, most of which were Mode 'A'.

The overall focus of the unit was to use 'off the job' training to encourage the personal development of the trainees. Experiential group learning was used as an aid to better decision making by trainees in the future. Some managing agents were sympathetic to this. They realised that a self reliant and confident worker was a good worker. The best example of this was Management Development Services Ltd in the retail area. They had 400 places in the South West, most in quite small shops. They had good supervisors who cared about trainees and they were enthusiastic about the approach of the YTS Unit. Other managing agents were very different. They wanted practical skills (narrowly defined) to be taught and they blamed the unit if the trainee had personal problems.

The YTS pilot schemes were given 26 weeks 'off the job' training. The first full year of YTS saw this reduced to 13 weeks. Some managing agents could not afford to buy the full 13 weeks from the unit; they were forced to provide some of this themselves. It was very hard to fit anything in, given the emphasis on practical skills. It was difficult to find the time to address health education issues.

Alcohol might be raised as an issue by trainees in a group discussion. It was more likely to be addressed only when it was a factor in poor performance or poor time keeping. Supervisors were likely to address such situations through individual counselling although some would have the confidence to initiate a group discussion. This type of trainee problem did not often arise. However, there was a strong ethos of heavy drinking amongst young men from council estates in the South of the city. Most drank in pubs from age 16 onwards. It was part of a lifestyle. Consideration needed to be given to alcohol in relation to this lifestyle rather than abstracted out. Such education needed to draw upon the actual experiences of the young people. Schooling, housing, employment prospects and lifestyle needed to be linked together. The head of the YTS training unit felt frustrated by the lack of time to attempt this. Young people from these council estates left school convinced they were failures. They had failed exams, and yet this was because lessons and curricula were so rarely relevant in content or style to the estate experiences of the young people.

(b)   The Community Programme project

This project was funded by the MSC as part of its Community Programme for the long term unemployed and was based in St. Aldhelms. The project was run by a charitable trust and it was possible to hold discussions with the manager and a sponsor. The project evolved out of a series of mock interviews being offered to fifth formers from local schools. It was felt that these interviews risked increasing frustration because the young people realised there was little chance of work. An action committee was formed and the present Community Programme project evolved. There were two task forces. One dealt with building and decorating for elderly residents. The other visited elderly residents as community aides. The project also ran a day centre for elderly people.

Both the manager and sponsor believed local people were proud of the project and felt it was 'theirs'. This included the workers who had worked without pay during weekends to help prepare a new day centre which was to be opened by the Lord Mayor. However, workers tended to arrive with a school mentality. They overslept; they messed about. At the project this led to a loss of pay and such behaviour was soon abandoned.

Alcohol was not seen as an important issue, despite the estate being a 'hard drinking area'. Drink had been available at the Lord Mayor's reception but no one had abused it. People drank to excess from boredom and depression. The project gave hope of a better future and so discouraged such behaviour; wages were too low, in any case, to leave much disposable income. The MSC was considering the introduction of a stronger training element into the Community Programme but they both felt this should concentrate upon practical rather than social skills.

(c)   The community worker and the residents' association

A local authority community worker on the estate was also visitied and he indicated that local drinking patterns were not something that caused him great concern. Heavy drinking was accepted and encouraged in the male population. It was a sign of being a 'proper bloke' and such behaviour was often encouraged in adolescent males by mothers and 'grannies'. In his ten years on the estate, however, he felt that there had been little increase in the amount of alcohol consumed. There were not many pubs on the estate and money was short. The massive rise in unemployment and growth in solvent abuse were far more important social changes in that period and both needed a concerted attack.

A lot of his time had recently been spent in helping to establish and support a new residents' association, which wished to take over the local authority owned social centre. Two committee members of this association were also seen. They explained how the association had grown out of a community festival which was celebrating the 50th anniversary of the estate. They were trying to tackle the despair created by unemployment. They wanted to provide activities appropriate to and affordable by unemployed people. Local residents needed encouragement to regain self confidence and to appreciate that everyone has something to give. Drink and solvent abuse were seen as a response to the pressures of bad housing and unemployment.

Alcohol education in St. Aldhelms and the South West programme

Table 22 indicates a similar situation to that in the other localities with regard to knowledge of the South West alcohol education programme. Of the 11 who had heard of the programme, seven had a city, county or district health authority function rather than a more local St. Aldhelms focus. One other was based in an adjacent neighbourhood. Of the remaining three, the community psychiatric nurse was keenly involved in work with solvent abuse in several areas including St. Aldhelms. The community worker had received a one page outline of the programme although he could not remember where it had come from; he had written asking for more

Table 22: Knowledge of the South West alcohol education programme

Subject area of respondent		Number of respond-ents	Aware of prog-ramme	Unaware of prog-ramme
1. Alcohol and specialist provison in the voluntary sector	a) Council on Alcoholism	2	2	0
	b) Self help groups	1	0	1
2. Alcohol and the NHS	a) Psychiatric services	2	2	0
	b) Health education	2	2	0
	c) Schools of nursing	5	0	5
	d) Primary health care	8	0	8
3. Counselling services and alcohol education	a) Statutory agencies	2	2	0
	b) Voluntary agencies	2	0	2
	c) The churches	1	0	1
4. Alcohol and the education department	a) Schools	7	1	6
	b) The youth service	7	1	6
	c) Colleges of further education	3	0	3
5. Alcohol and the law	a) Police	2	0	2
	b) Magistrates	1	0	1
6. Miscellaneous	a) Youth Training Scheme	2	0	2
	b) Community Programme project	2	0	2
	c) Community worker and residents association	3	1	2
TOTALS		52	11	41

162

information but had received no reply. The final officer was a social worker who was heavily involved in various aspects of alcohol counselling and education.

The discussions were spread over six months, from December 1984 to May 1985, although the vast majority did not take place until April and May. Lack of knowledge and awareness of the South West alcohol education programme was perhaps not surprising. It had not then been publicly launched in the county. An important test of the programme will be whether there has been much change in this situation when the research team return to this locality in about 18 months' time.

Respondents were also asked about whether they were sympathetic to the aims of the programme. General attitudes to alcohol education have already been characterised, but it is worth taking a closer look at comments about the programme and its launch from the 11 professionals who were already aware of its existence. Two were uncritical enthusiasts; the programme would help to put alcohol education on the agenda, which they had been trying to achieve for some years. Two felt it sounded an excellent idea from their limited knowledge. One was sympathetic towards the philosophy of the programme, but stressed that the success of social education in schools was more dependent upon the form and philosophy of the teaching rather than the chosen content area. Another believed that there was an enormously important role for alcohol education, but recognition was required that controlled drinking was not an option for certain types of problem drinker. Similar views were expressed by another, combined with a concern that making education a priority could be linked to a decline in resources for treatment. Three of the remaining officers expressed belief in the philosophy of the programme, but felt that the programme faced important organisational problems. All three felt that objectives and targeted groups (professionals or consumers) needed to be more clearly defined. One of them felt that there had been inadequate recognition of previous and existing alcohol education activities. The remaining officer was the least sympathetic to the philosophy and aims of the programme. He felt there was a need for alcohol education, but that its primary focus should be encouraging abstinence, especially among young people.

Overall, the St. Aldhelms locality study was the most interesting because of the extent to which alcohol education networks had developed prior to the launch of the South West programme. The director of the Council on Alcoholism and a health education officer (HEO) have been heavily involved in various alcohol education and <u>Drinkwatch</u> initiatives. The Council has an education officer who is able to make a contribution to a wide range of events. There is a growing network of alcohol abuse forums in the county. Two district health authorities are considering the establishment of an HEO post with alcohol education in the job description.

This has been further underlined by the new policy and strategic plan of the Council on Alcoholism which was developing during the period of the fieldwork. This draws together many of the themes discussed by the director in the last annual report. The plan is based upon a framework of four principles, initially agreed by the Executive Committee in December, 1984. These were:

(a)   The Council on Alcoholism is an agency which promotes policies which minimise the harmful consequences of drinking alcohol.

(b)   The Council on Alcoholism promotes policies which take into account the social and environmental factors contributing to alcohol misuse and its consequences.

(c)   The Council on Alcoholism promotes policies which lead to the greater involvement of the community in providing services which minimise the consequences of the misuse of alcohol.

(d)   The Council on Alcoholism is an agency which promotes sensible drinking.

The aims and objectives of the Council on Alcoholism seem increasingly consistent with the philosophy of the South West alcohol education programme. The emphasis on "the social and environmental factors contributing to alcohol misuse and its consequences" is perhaps most significant, because of the recognition of the need to attract the interest and involvement of a wide community of professionals, many of whom will be highly suspicious of narrow medical definitions of the problem.

However, the inclusion of more professionals and local residents in the debate about alcohol and alcohol misuse is hard to achieve, as can be shown by a close look at the alcohol abuse forum in the South of the city. The research team has not attended any of its meetings and so comments are based upon discussions with members and minutes of some of the meetings. The fourth meeting was attended by 14 members and there were two apologies. However, two of those present were from the Council on Alcoholism and so have no specific focus on that part of the city. One member has since retired, and another has left the area because of promotion. Three of those present indicated to the research team that they did not expect to become regular members; the two welfare counsellors from the technical college did not expect to become regular attenders at the forum. They were interested to find out more about service availability, but the forum was seen as having too narrow a focus to justify their regular attendance. There were no community representatives at the meeting while the statutory and voluntary sector 'professionals' tended to be from agencies concerned with families with social problems (social workers, probation officers and education welfare officers) rather than those that provide a service for the general population (GPs, teachers and health visitors). Our perception was that its continuance depended upon the involvement of those already heavily engaged in the politics of alcohol education and counselling.

Existing members of the forum recognised these difficulties and they had already decided to seek a much wider representation from local professionals. The director of the Council on Alcoholism later stressed that other forums had shown that this is a long process but one that could be successful; a forum in another part of the county now had wide membership, its own strategic plan and was an active influence upon local policy developments.

The South West alcohol education programme faces many of the same dilemmas as these forums. How can the influence of the programme be made to penetrate far down hierarchies, in a way that involves many more professionals than just those with a prior interest in the area? How can you engage the interest, commitment and understanding of those professionals who do not have a prior involvement in the area?

Drinking patterns and problems in St. Aldhelms

Many professionals in this study were convinced that St. Aldhelms did have a tradition of excessive drinking. This was mainly seen as being composed of male beer drinkers who would perceive the consumption of five or six pints per night as 'normal'. This behaviour was taking place despite the fact that the estate had very few public houses. There was no consensus as to whether such consumption had decreased or increased as a result of high rates of unemployment. Some believed that the despair of unemployment

165

drove people to drink. Others stressed that unemployment reduced the household income and so restricted the opportunity to drink.

There was a far less coherent view of female drinking on the estate and the extent to which alcohol was kept in the home. Some saw the estate as the kind where men drank in the pub and women stayed at home to look after the children; such women were far more likely to be addicted to tranquillisers than alcohol. Others took the opposite view and stressed that nearly every family had a drinks cabinet, irrespective of household poverty, and that this encouraged excessive drinking among all family members.

Nearly all respondents agreed on two points. The first was that it would be very difficult to address alcohol consumption on the estate without addressing the more general issues of deprivation such as low income, bad housing and high unemployment. Some respondents seemed to see local residents as suffering from certain inherent weaknesses which explained their poor material circumstances; the majority were concerned that residents were vulnerable to stigma and that alcohol education on poor estates could easily appear to 'blame the victim'. The second point was an overwhelming concern with the collapse of morale among young people on the estate. They rejected school. They consumed illegal drugs and solvents. They lacked recreational facilities on the estate and they lacked the financial resources to seek such facilities elsewhere. Above all, they were experiencing despair because of the lack of future job prospects. They were often characterised as being 'strong in the arm and thick in the head' in the same way as 'born and bred' residents in Westcross and Breaton. Many remarked that young people were increasingly combining solvent abuse with drink, especially cider.

References

1. Lovering, J. (1985), 'Regional intervention, defence industries and the structuring of space in Britain', Society and Space, Vol 3, pp 83-107.

2. This is discussed in more detail in Franklin, A. (1985), Pub drinking and the licensed trade: a study of drinking cultures and local community in two areas of South West England,

School for Advanced Urban Studies, University of Bristol, Occasional Paper No. 21.

3. Osborn, A., Leckie, T., Bardell, L. and Lamont, F. (1980), <u>Alcohol related problems in current social work cases,</u> Lothian Regional Social Work Department.

4. The research team are grateful to the author of this dissertation for permission to draw on his work without the usual full reference.

5. During the period of fieldwork, the youth service in the county ceased to be a part of the responsibilities of the education department and was transferred to become part of a new community leisure department.   An interesting discussion of the implications of this kind of move can be found in Holland, M. (1985), 'Education or leisure - whose move next', <u>Youth in Society,</u> June, pp 11-13.

6. Lord Scarman (1982 edition), <u>The Scarman report: the Brixton disorders, 10-12 April 1981,</u> Pelican.

6

ALCOHOL EDUCATION IN THE SOUTH WEST: THEMES AND ISSUES FROM THE FOUR LOCALITY STUDIES

Introduction

Chapter 1 outlined the lessons that had been learnt from the Tyne Tees campaign and how these had been incorporated into the statement of the aims and philosophy of the South West alcohol education programme. The next four chapters looked at how a wide range of professionals in four contrasting communities conceptualised alcohol education in relation to their day-to-day work. This material provides a backdrop against which to explore some of the difficulties and dilemmas that will be faced by the South West programme in its attempt to engage the active long term involvement and commitment of such workers to alcohol education.

What is meant by local patterns of drinking?

One of the lessons from the previous Tyne Tees campaign appeared to be the importance of recognising and responding to local patterns of drinking. The locality study approach adopted by the research team reflected an attempt to respond to this lesson. At the end of each of the last four chapters, common themes about drinking patterns in these communities are presented. In so doing, the research team were far from sure whether these represented an accurate picture of local communities or a commentary about male middle class fantasies about the behaviour of women, elderly people and working class families.

One method for improving this situation would be to carry out detailed research on drinking patterns in the South West. However, although research of this kind is clearly needed, care must be taken not to become too seduced by the concept of 'local'. Would a study of drinking behaviour by unemployed working class youth on a council estate in Gloucester be irrelevant to those working with similar groups in Bristol, Cheltenham, Exeter, Plymouth, Taunton, Bridgwater or any of the smaller market towns?

This study underlined the enormous problem of defining what is meant by the term 'local'. The related concepts of community and neighbourhood have generated an enormous amount of research, debate and argument since the earliest years of sociological research.[1] Chapter 1 stated that a region was too large and diverse an area to have one local style of drinking. However, this raises the question of whether the appropriate size is the town, the village, the estate or whatever. Two examples can be given from the locality case studies to illustrate this point. First, most people would perceive St. Aldhelms as being a homogeneous interwar council estate. However, this is not the case from the point of view of field level professionals or local residents. Different parts of the estate are seen as 'rough' or 'respectable'; council house allocation policies are seen as influencing this situation. The 'respectable' parts of the estate are seen as having a stable population, strong informal social control, limited illegal drug consumption and 'respectable' patterns of alcohol consumption. The opposite is seen as true for other parts of the estate. Second, the fishing village (Lyncombe) in Chapter 4 is very small and yet it contains a bewildering number of social groups. There are fishing families, retired couples and newcomers who own the local tourist businesses. The local GP stressed the very different attitudes to drink between younger and older elements of the community, the latter still being influenced by the hostility of Methodism towards drink. No single message about drinking would be appropriate or relevant to all members of that community.

One reason for this complexity is that the cultural specificity of the locality is not the only variable that has to be considered. Social class, gender and age group[2] may be even more relevant. It can be argued that the most significant difference between Westcross and St. Aldhelms is not 'cultural' but rather the availability of manual work in one area and its absence in the other. Alcohol education programmes may, therefore, need to think of targeting specific groups within several communities rather than as targeting communities as such. The Tyne Tees campaign, particularly the Bellamy advertisements, did not address all drinkers but certain types of drinker, namely male beer drinkers.

Third, there is a danger of alcohol education programmes such as the one in the South West becoming disabled by too much focus on the complexity of local patterns of drinking. The fishing village example does not indicate the need for yet more sophisticated research to uncover 'the truth' about drinking variations in the region before the programme can proceed. Different types of intervention require different levels of detailed knowledge. Uncovering variations in very local drinking practices can best be achieved by professionals developing the confidence to talk to local people about why they have developed particular styles of drinking. This is consistent with the emphasis of the programme upon participative learning. Dorn, in Alcohol, youth and the state, [3] provides a clear example of how that could be achieved in schools:

"A health education curriculum based on a materialist approach to youth cultures and health-related practices therein would involve an investigation - carried out jointly by pupils and teachers - of the material preconditions and forms of local youth cultures.... Having identified pupils' culture, discussion could then move on to the ways in which health-related social practices - involving not only drinking, but eating, sexuality, etc - arise in each culture."

In this respect, the research team was impressed by the comprehensive school in one of the localities that made detailed use of the general health questionnaire developed by John Balding[4] at the School Health Education Unit, University of Exeter. This questionnaire offers the opportunity for teachers to discuss health related issues in a way that starts from the actual behaviour of young people rather than from an emphasis upon the need to encourage certain types of behaviour.

The second stage is to encourage young people to explain the meaning of such behaviour and how it relates to other aspects of their local youth cultures.

An alternative approach is that offered by Franklin in Pub drinking and the licensed trade[5] which provides a guide to how participant observation can be used in public houses on a systematic basis to obtain a more rounded impression of how drink is actually consumed in different communities and in different parts of different communities. An interest in and concern about local patterns of drinking implies a need to know far more than just how much is consumed and what is consumed. It implies a need to tackle the questions of how, why and in what context.

This complexity has perhaps been best illustrated in the research on The pub and the people[6] carried out by Mass-Observation just before the Second World War. This study looked at drinking patterns and behaviour in all the public houses in a Northern mill town. At the beginning of the report it lists the things that people do in pubs:[7]

SIT and/or STAND
DRINK
TALK about betting; sport; work; people; drinking; weather;
    politics; dirt
THINK
SMOKE
SPIT

Many PLAY GAMES: cards; dominoes, darts; quoits

Many BET: receive and pay out losings and winnings

PEOPLE SING AND LISTEN TO SINGING: PLAY THE PIANO AND LISTEN TO IT BEING PLAYED; THESE THINGS ARE OFTEN CONNECTED WITH PUBS....

    weddings and funerals
    quarrels and fights
    bowls, fishing and picnics
    trade unions
    secret societies   Oddfellows   Buffs
    religious processions
    sex
    getting jobs
    crime and prostitution
    dog shows
    pigeon flying

PEOPLE SELL AND BUY: bootlaces; hot pies; black puddings; embrocation

Also: LOTTERIES AND SWEEPSTAKES happen; PREJUDICES gather

This study later discusses the meaning of all these activities to pub drinkers in the following words:

> "The pub with its essential factor alcohol provides for many Worktowners an alternative to the social groups and corporate beliefs of religion or politics, though not necessarily one exclusive to either interest. Religion

and politics depend on some desire, however small, to shape, or maintain the shape, of present and future, and the continuum is 'idealism'; the release, the immediate satisfaction, is 'the feeling of goodness', feeling good, personally and socially. The pub provides a lot of this. Through its liquors it shapes the future in one's mind, does so more personally by obliterating it and emphasizing goodness only of and in the present, with hope and thought stretching out no further than the edges of 'last hour' or 'closing time'. Drink, like its mythology of Lethe and Bacchus, is in this subtle sense a philosophy and ideology almost on its own account, and its feelings are not far from some of those in religion - particularly in religious conversion and absolutism. There is a lot more than drinking involved in drinking.[8]

The research team recognises that these quotations can be criticised on numerous grounds. First, they minimise the harm that often results from extensive pub drinking. Second, these quotations seem to assume that alcohol is essential if the other activities of the public house are to be enjoyed. Third, it is dangerous to equate alcohol consumption with public houses. The public house has declined as an institution since the days of the Worktown study - the Wilson study estimated that for men on average 26% of drinking occasions were in the home and this proportion rose to 39% for women.[9]

However, the Worktown study and the research by Franklin do provide crucial insights into the meaning of alcohol in our society and why it will be difficult for the South West alcohol education programme to challenge existing drinking patterns. How many 'professionals' fully understand alcohol and its meaning to consumers?

The health and social costs of alcohol

The primary concern of many of our respondents, however, was not with the meaning to local residents of their drinking behaviour but rather a desire for data on the relationship of alcohol consumption to a variety of health and social problems. In Chapter 1, it was pointed out that authors such as Saunders[10] claimed that alcohol was "variously associated with" such diverse difficulties as throat cancer, accidental drowning, divorce and child abuse.

But what is meant by "variously associated with"? To what extent does this imply a causal or partially causal relationship? With the kind of list provided by Saunders, the importance of the relationship between alcohol and the problem will be more clearcut in some instances than others. The impact of alcohol upon driving ability is clearly defined and the resultant risk is incurred as much by pedestrians and other drivers as by the drinking driver.[11] There is a clear need to challenge the existing complacency about the leniency offered to drunken drivers, and the South West alcohol education programme - backed up by local data - could be an ideal mechanism to perform this task. Indeed, the known physiological effects of alcohol clearly place consumers at risk from a variety of potential accidents in the home, in the workplace, on the road or in the water. There is considerable scope and need to develop an alcohol and safety strand to the programme.

However, the causal relationship becomes more problematic when one moves into the area of alcohol and those illnesses and health problems where the impact and importance of alcohol may be less clearcut than with the most recognised alcohol related illnesses (eg cirrhosis). The extent of the research task involved in unravelling the alcohol-specific component in various cancers and in birth abnormalities is enormously complex. This has recently been underlined by the research of Moira Plant on the foetal alcohol syndrome.[12] Medical advice to pregnant women has increasingly veered towards the need for abstinence or near abstinence if the risk of a birth abnormality from alcohol consumption is to be avoided. However, Plant's four year study of 1,000 pregnant women has led her to conclude that:

> "....although maternal drinking is <u>associated</u> with some birth abnormalities it does not appear to <u>cause</u> them. Instead alcohol consumption during pregnancy appears to serve as a 'marker' for other, more potent, influences. Certainly if the risk of a substance being harmful to the baby is raised, accepted and indeed acceptable medical policy, is usually to warn against use at any level. However a number of the studies carried out on moderate to low levels of alcohol consumption have not shown that alcohol in small amounts is harmful to the unborn child."[13]

In other words, the heavy drinker whose child has a birth abnormality is also likely to be a heavy smoker, live in bad housing, have an inadequate diet and suffer general symptoms of mental stress. Plant's conclusion is that alcohol is a 'marker' rather than a major causal influence in many birth abnormalities in such families. Other interpretations of the research results might be made and some of these have already been offered in the letters page of the journal Alcohol Concern[14] by correspondents who believe a definite 'no' is still the correct advice to expectant mothers.

Such questions can be tackled only by lengthy and quite specialised research. Even then it may prove impossible to come to clear conclusions because of the complexity of the issues involved. Seely[15] in a recent review of the research on food related diseases concluded that "a century of research has so far failed to identify the cause of any one of them". Additives, salt, sugar and saturated fats have all come under suspicion but research has been unable to disentangle one element of diet from all the others. The dilemma is whether such research 'clears' alcohol or merely illustrates the limitations of present investigative techniques.

The causal relationship issue may be equally problematic when one considers such social problems as murder, divorce, burglary and child abuse. An emphasis upon alcohol as causing or precipitating such problems can represent a heavy over-simplification of a complex social situation. Respondents often claimed that working class youth broke the law on certain estates because they had been involved in heavy drinking. Gill, in his excellent account of Luke Street: housing policy, conflict and the creation of the delinquent area[16], outlines the following ten stages in the growth of delinquency on a Merseyside interwar council estate:

(i) Luke Street in the 1950s relatively 'quiet' in terms of adolescent 'trouble'. Large families of original tenants grown up and left and so a degree of under-occupation of homes in the neighbourhood.

(ii) From late 1950s onwards arrival in Luke Street of very large families. Therefore, disproportionate number of young children in the neighbourhood.

(iii) These families already facing difficulties in achieving required 'standards' in 'coping' and in 'making ends meet'.

(iv) Children growing up in a public setting because of over-crowding in the home, lack of organised recreational facilities in the neighbourhood.

(v)   Public nature of lives of young people in neighbourhood leads to beginning of small-scale local vandalism and 'trouble' on the streets.

(vi)   Effects of this exacerbated for older groups by high level of adolescent unemployment.

(vii)   Because of this a 'tradition' of conflict with the police grows up in the neighbourhood.

(viii) External stereotype or 'reputation' of area developed by mid-1960s and begins to have amplifying effect on difficulties faced by young people in the neighbourhood.

(ix)   Self-perpetuating process of increase in number of incidents and 'trouble'.

(x)   Stereotyping as 'lawless' leads to more police surveillance and increased police attention to certain forms of public behaviour on the part of young people in the area.

Several respondents in the locality studies said there was a need for shock/horror data on alcohol and social problems. Resource holders often make it clear that alcohol education will not receive more resources and higher priority unless such evidence can be produced. However, the South West alcohol education programme needs to be sure that claimed linkages between alcohol and social problems can be justified, especially to the uncommitted who may feel there is a wilful refusal to consider other factors.

One way forward is to use local data to develop a dialogue and debate with South West professionals about these complex issues. Nobody knows how much crime, child abuse and marital disharmony is caused by alcohol and we suspect human behaviour is too complex for social research to provide a definitive answer. It can indicate the percentage of cases where high alcohol consumption appears to be present and it can indicate the percentage of cases where this appears to be of potential causal importance. However, such research may often be based on the records and files of local authority and health authority organisations, and it needs to be borne in mind that these may represent the prejudices and anxieties of the reporter as much as the actual behaviour of the client, consumer or patient.

A social worker who produces a court report in connection with care proceedings on a young child is doing much more than just presenting the 'facts'. He or she is also making an argument that

175

attempts to justify the recommendations of the report. The presentation (or non-presentation) of the drinking behaviour of the parents must be understood in this context.[17] Our locality studies underlined the extent to which the selective presentation of 'facts' can be a controversial issue in the area of alcohol and crime. Probation officers in two of the studies mentioned the high percentage of social enquiry reports that referred to alcohol as a problem area for their clients. However, two magistrates and one consultant psychiatrist expressed some anger that claiming a drink problem could be used to justify criminal activity. Two examples were found of probation initiatives to establish alcohol education groups for alcohol dependent clients being met with some misapprehension from others. Local data on alcohol and crime could be used to facilitate a debate about the complex relationship between the two rather than as a simplistic statement of how much crime is actually caused by alcohol.

We are not denying that increasing alcohol consumption is "variously associated with" the growth of a whole host of health and social problems. However, the importance of the words "variously associated with" should not be lost, especially when attempting to engage the interest of others who may be concerned about how many of these same problems are associated with a variety of other factors such as low income, unemployment, bad housing, urban design, work stress, gender stereotypes or whatever. Both sides need to learn from each other if a meaningful attempt is to be made to tackle many of these complex health and social problems.

We suspect that much of our readership will feel these comments to be rather negative and offering too few clues as to how to proceed. We will, therefore, end this section by offering an illustration of the kind of research and policy initiative that does meet our strictures. The Home Office has recently produced a report on Implementing crime prevention measures by Tim Hope.[18] One chapter of this report provides a policy analysis of drinking and disorder in city centres. The author does not make any sweeping statements about how the immediate vicinities of all public houses experience a high rate of crime. Instead, he shows how 'occurrence logs'[19] were used by the police in Newcastle to pinpoint how public disorder is associated with particular public houses in particular areas of the city centre at particular times of the evening. Three troublespots were defined, namely four streets that had twelve pubs, the entrance area to two adjacent nightclubs and the metro 'rail' system. The research of the police had, therefore, shown that the bulk of this disorder was time-specific (ie incidents concentrated markedly at the weekends and at the end of permitted drinking hours) and it was location-specific (ie certain premises and public spaces had more disorder than others). The disorder that occurred at these times in these places was not solely the result of the volume of alcohol consumed by the culprits and victims. Instead the determinants were complex and included the socio-cultural norms and practices of the customer, the inter-personal skills of bar staff in dealing with potentially aggressive customers, the physical location of particular drinking outlets and the design of the city centre.

Table 23: Possible measures for preventing drink related disorders in city centres

1. General disorderliness

a. Sentencing to deter offenders
b. General health education and specific treatment of persons 'at risk' of heavy drinking and disorderliness
c. Social reforms to affect the 'root causes' of heavy drinking and violence

2. Time-specific disorderliness

a. Alter permitted hours - extend, abandon, or selectively stagger pub closing times to avoid a concentration of drinkers inside pubs and on the street
b. Increase the number of late-night premises through permissive licensing - to achieve the same effect as (a) but under somewhat more restrictive controls (ie special hours certificates)
c. Increase police supervision of premises and public spaces at closing time to match the greater need for control
d. Train bar staff in interpersonal relations and management techniques - to lower the risk of confrontation with customers at closing time
e. Facilitate the dispersal of people from the city centre - increase public transport provision to speed the removal of people and avoid the gathering of disruptive crowds.

177

3.   Situation-specific disorderliness

a.   Revoke licences or impose conditions on premises which have a record of disorder
b.   Alter the number and density of licensed premises
c.   Alter the character of pubs and clubs - encourage the development of premises where the facilities are unlikely to lead to disorder
d.   Discourage youth-oriented and age-specific leisure activity and facilities from concentrating in city centres
e.   Improve the ability of bar staff to cope with disorder, through better training and management practice
f.   Encourage management practices that will result in the keeping of orderly premises
g.   Improve the ability of the police to supervise licensed premises and respond to disorder
h.   Reduce the amount of indefensible public space in city centres by urban planning and design.[20]

This analysis enables Hope to provide a list of possible measures for preventing drink related disorders in the city centres (see Table 23), the feasibility of which are then discussed. Hope is thus able to show how the choice of a preventive strategy needs to be linked to the dimensions of specific local situations. He also illustrates how the concerns of alcohologists may overlap with those of professionals with expertise in other areas. The list supplied by Hope recognises the concern of many professionals about the importance of public transport policy and of sensitive urban design.

The latter issue is especially topical at the moment due to the publicity given to Utopia on trial by Coleman[21] which attempts to prove a link between the design of public housing and local levels of crime, child abuse and general ill health. It is argued that good estates reduce these problems; bad estates worsen them. The obsessional pursuit of these ideas can also, of course, undermine the development of a dialogue amongst a wide range of professionals, who will have differing ideas about causative health relationships. This brings us back to the issue of policy implementation.

A 'bottom up' approach to policy implementation?

An important finding from the Tyne Tees evaluation was the need for a 'bottom up' approach to future regional programmes. In Tyne Tees, the HEC upset local professionals by the failure to consult. The programme appeared to be imposed on the North East. Many of these previous mistakes have been avoided in the South West and programme management is more clearly situated within the region. However, the locality studies indicate that three crucial issues need to be addressed:

(a)   The relationship of Key Tutor networks, health education officers and Councils on Alcoholism.

(b)   The relationship of residents to local groups run by professionals.

(c)   The relationship of the majority of field level professionals to the South West alcohol education programme.

(a)   The tension between Key Tutor networks, health education officers and Councils on Alcoholism is present in all four locality studies. This tension is not an abnormal or unusual feature of organisational life. At a recent <u>Drug questions</u>[22] seminar, a researcher in the heroin field spoke of how he had been invited to talk to a new committee in Hull that was attempting to co-ordinate all those concerned with illegal drugs in that community. The researcher was asked to stress the need for and importance of co-operation and co-ordination. He chose instead to tell them that they would all 'fall out' within a few months because of their very different perspectives on the drug problem. They had to learn how to continue talking to each other despite these differences. Such tensions can easily be exacerbated by competition, either real or imagined, between such organisations for limited resources.

However, it is possible to reduce these conflicts and tensions through a clearer recognition of the pressures faced by small voluntary organisations. More could have been done in this respect in the South West. In Tyne Tees the North East Council on Alcoholism was largely created as a result of the HEC campaign. Its success and growth was identified with the success and growth of the campaign. In the South West, there are seven Councils on Alcoholism, all in very different stages of development. In Cornford the South West programme and the Key Tutor courses were seen as representing a chance for the local Council on Alcoholism to establish itself on a much firmer financial and staffing footing. Interested professionals could attend these courses and then return to help in a collective effort to develop alcohol education. There was a shared agenda to raise the priority and visibility of alcohol education within the area. This is a very different situation from that of the more established councils, some of whom were already moving into prevention and education prior to the arrival of the programme.

The Action Plan, however, spoke of the formation of "a network of Key Tutors throughout the South West with local teams within each Health District".. The potential relationship of these teams to either Executive Committees of the Councils of Alcoholism or to existing alcohol abuse forums is not explored. Small voluntary organisations survive by persuading local authorities and health authorities to supply grants. The argument for the grant is made by reference to the size of the local alcohol problem and quality of work already being carried out. The 'ownership' of alcohol education events can, therefore, be crucial. If many of the Key Tutors are involved with the Council or sit on the Executive Committee, who will be seen as 'owning' the future activities? Similar points can be made in relation to funding of health education officers with alcohol education in their job description. These posts are to be welcomed but they need to be developed in a way that complements rather than threatens education initiatives in the voluntary sector.

(b)   The HEC emphasises the importance of a 'holistic' approach to health in which ordinary people have a right to define what they value about different lifestyles. In other words, professionals should not impose their own concepts of 'healthy living' on others. The South West programme needs to be clear about the distinction between local groups of professionals and local groups of residents, especially when statements are made about 'what the community wants' in relation to such issues as local policing and licensing strategies.

The encouragement of a 'moral panic' about alcohol related problems in the South West may help to release much needed funds and the 'panic' may be based upon the existence of a massive problem that existing statutory agencies are refusing to confront. And yet many of the comments from the middle class professionals in the four studies underline the temptation to equate alcohol abuse with low income working class families. A 'moral panic' that focuses down upon alcohol abuse in some sections of the population but ignores it in others is something that must be avoided. In this respect, it should be noted that members of Councils on Alcoholism were the least likely to make this mistake - they are only too aware of the prevalence of alcohol abuse problems in all sections of the community.

(c)   Many of the comments in this final chapter have focused on the tactics of how to engage the interest and commitment of the vast bulk of professionals in the South West who have previously expressed little enthusiasm or knowledge about alcohol education. Can the South West alcohol education programme incorporate many of these people into local networks of alcohol education? In this respect, there is a real danger that new initiatives will mainly attract those already committed to the importance of alcohol education.

As indicated in other chapters, a frequent tactic of the 'committed' is to encourage the involvement of key policy makers and resource holders from their local communities.   The composition of some Executive Committees of Councils on Alcoholism is an excellent example of this.   The South West alcohol education programme is faced with the same dilemma as Councils on Alcoholism.   The programme needs to engage the active support of key resource holders. Alcohol education needs to be recognised at a policy level by local authorities and district health authorities.   They are most likely to make a positive response if they are convinced that alcohol can be clearly shown to cause specific health and social problems, together with an estimation of the financial implications for those authorities.   The ongoing debate in the Cornford locality study is perhaps the best example of this.

However, the resultant policies then have to be implemented. Such implementation can easily be blocked by what the American literature tends to refer to as "street level bureaucrats".[23]   The tactical question faced by the programme is how to minimise these blockages and how to engage the attention and interest of the vast bulk of professional staff who have no great interest in alcohol education at the present. The tradition amongst alcohol educators and alcohol researchers is to attempt to prove that such professionals are: (a) ignorant about the volume of alcohol misuse in society and (b) anxious about their role adequacy, role legitimacy and role support in tackling such problems.   This approach is based upon the pioneering research of Shaw et al in Responding to drinking problems.[24] Many of those involved with the South West programme believe in this approach. Much of the material collected for the locality studies supports the findings of Shaw et al. Social workers, for example, need to be aware that alcohol can be a factor in child abuse situations. They need confidence in how to spot such 'clues', training in how to respond and the certainty of institutional support. Our research also underlined how the anxiety of some professionals about addressing alcohol issues with their clients sprang from an unease about their own drinking patterns. This unease endorses the relevance of potential alcohol educators attending Key Tutor courses in order to explore their own attitudes towards drink, and not just to acquire facts about alcohol.

However, as already outlined, the locality studies also indicate the need to avoid just 'talking down' to other professionals. The Drinking choices manual stresses the need for participative and experiential teaching. The research team understands this to mean that the teacher and the taught both have things to learn. Is this consistent with just bombarding professional workers in the South West with facts on alcohol and crime, alcohol and divorce, alcohol and child abuse, etc? Do these professionals have anything to tell alcohologists about the importance of other factors in social problem causation? Is there a danger that the uncommitted will ignore or reject the programme if it appears too 'obsessive' about alcohol in a way that denies the complex relationship of one factor to another in social problem causation?

Targeting professionals

One mechanism for reducing this problem is for the South West alcohol education programme to become more sophisticated in how it targets different professionals. A commitment to inter-disciplinary work does not mean that differences between professional groups can be ignored. Why do probation officers tend to talk about alcohol and crime? Why do social workers talk about alcohol and child abuse? Why do teachers talk about alcohol and young people? The answer is obviously that organisational role and professional training influence perceptions of the potential role for alcohol education. Such views can be challenged - but they do need to be understood.

Below is a fairly crude attempt to set out some of the differences between the professional groups in the four studies. There was no consensus on views within groups. Locality factors and personal views were also important. The respondents do not represent a carefully chosen sample, whose representativeness can be guaranteed. The characterisations below, therefore, offer a limited contribution to a debate about how the South West programme can engage the maximum interest of the maximum number of professionals in a way that is consistent with the philosophy of the programme. The overall finding, however, was the enormous gap between knowledge, attitudes and behaviour of professionals on the ground and the objectives of the alcohol education programme. The South West programme has an enormous task ahead. The research team believes that this task will be manageable, given the limited resources available, only if some hard targeting and priority decisions are made.

Consultant psychiatrists and community psychiatric nurses

Their focus is normally on the treatment of people with severe drinking problems. Their interest in prevention and education, therefore, tends to be on persuading problem drinkers to come forward at an earlier stage, and ensuring adequate resources to enable problem drinkers to develop control over their alcohol consumption.

Health education officers

Many of these officers have been influenced by the same educational ideas about experiential and participative learning that underpin the philosophy of the programme and the Drinking choices manual. However, their involvement in the programme remains problematic for at least three reasons:

1. Their numbers are small and several have been in post only a short time so that they are still preoccupied with establishing their health education departments. Unlike the North East, there is no well established regional network of HEOs who are used to working together.

2. Their health promotion responsibilities are enormous. Few HEOs would deny the importance of alcohol education but several may find it difficult to perceive how they can create more space for this work. One solution to such multiple pressure is to 'hive off' certain health topics to specialist voluntary organisations. If a decision to do this in the area of alcohol education has already been made, a message that they and their health authority should take more direct responsibility for this area may be seen as problematic.

3. HEOs perceive work priorities as evolving out of a complex set of negotiations, primarily within their health authority. They may object to the arrival of a new priority - alcohol education - from outside this area.

183

Nurses and nurse education

The research team was unable to uncover any consistent pattern to alcohol education for nurses at a local level. Detailed written curricula on training are often difficult to obtain. Alcohol education in most instances means a visit to the local treatment unit or a speaker from AA. Some notable exceptions to this were found, especially the nurse educator in Cornford who has been on a Key Tutor course. At the same time there is a growing interest in the issue of work stress within nurse education and this should clearly include a consideration of excessive drinking, particularly for in-service training for nurse managers, to enable them to monitor this danger in their nursing staff.

Primary health care

The response of GPs and health visitors was perhaps the most disappointing in relation to alcohol education. There were grumbles about the lack of treatment facilities. Little interest was expressed in the relationship of alcohol to physical illnesses other than liver cirrhosis. They emphasised that the bulk of their work was crisis intervention with individuals. One GP said he was not paid to carry out preventive work. The health visitors were often interested in the South West programme but found it difficult to grasp its philosophy and approach.

Social workers and probation officers

Their interest in alcohol - when it existed - was in relation to their statutory responsibilities. Probation officers were often very interested in the relationship of crime and alcohol. Social workers were far more interested in alcohol as a factor in child abuse situations. Both groups tend not to be interested in general health promotion. Social workers and probation officers varied enormously in the extent to which they believed that alcohol was a significant factor in leading their clients to require professional help.

Samaritans and marriage guidance counsellors

The Samaritans saw themselves as 'listening posts' that have no active role to play in alcohol education, other than supporting callers to seek help elsewhere. Relationships are the focus of marriage guidance counsellors. Alcohol would be addressed as and when appropriate but there was little support for the view that this was a topic that required special emphasis in their training.

Teachers and schools

Health education and social education varied enormously in how it was taught in the various schools in the four localities. Some teachers and advisers had been influenced by the same educational models as used by the South West alcohol education programme. Various School Council projects[25] had been very influential upon these teachers, and this could especially be seen in the interviews with the pastoral adviser in the St. Aldhelms study and the teacher at the comprehensive school who made extensive use of the general health questionnaire developed by John Balding, though such teachers are a minority. They also tend to stress the importance of process rather than content. In other words, the successful use of participative techniques and the encouragement of the capacity to make personal lifestyle decisions is seen as more important than whether this is attempted through a detailed consideration of alcohol, solvents, illegal drugs, smoking or diet.

The majority of teachers, however, are still involved in a much more didactic and prescriptive approach in which young people are warned about the dangers of certain types of behaviour. Health education is often addressed in a fairly incoherent way through a variety of subjects supplied by a variety of teachers, many of whom will be chosen because they have the 'space' to take on further teaching commitments. Health education lacks status within schools because it is not an examinable subject.

However, there are some positive features to the interviews in schools. First, schools are reconsidering health and social education and many are moving to a more structured curriculum, which is to be made available to all ability ranges.[26] Second, this group of professionals is very keen to obtain pamphlets, posters and videos on alcohol education; they are very interested in the South West programme.

Youth workers

Youth workers could be split up into two main groups. The 'traditionalists' see themselves as running recreational facilities for young people; their main task is to discourage trouble makers, including under age drinkers. The second group are those who subscribe to the main objectives outlined by the 1982 review of the youth service in England:

> "There is virtual unanimity that the fundamental purpose of the Youth Service is to provide programmes

of personal development comprising, in shorthand terms, social and political education.... We repeat here that we see social education as essentially an experiential process, as opposed to the passive reception of ideas, impressions and norms. It involves experimentation - the trying out of modes of behaviour and styles of action in a way calculated to help young individuals to know themselves and be able to cope with....the society of which they find themselves a part. From this premise it follows that the process of social education must above all be participatory."[27]

This approach is far more likely to be in evidence in urban than rural areas since only the former are likely to have many full time workers. There was little evidence apart from one in-service course in the St. Aldhelms case study that youth workers receive any training on alcohol education.

YTS trainers

The Youth Training Scheme has been in operation since May 1983 and is meant to offer a bridge from school to work for young people. There has been a fierce debate about the real objectives of this scheme (eg reducing unemployment figures, reducing wage expectations of young people, etc) but one objective stated in the Manpower Services Commission's 1982 Youth Task Group Report[28] was the failure of schools to realise the potential of many young people. YTS includes 13 week 'off the job' training in which young people can be taught a variety of both practical skills and life/social skills. This training may be supplied in a number of different ways, including through private sector trainers and lecturers in colleges of further education. Many of these trainers are likely to be sympathetic to the experiential models of educational learning, but all of the locality study respondents stressed how life/social skills training was being squeezed by the growing emphasis from the MSC and employers on the need to concentrate upon practical skills. Social skills issues are consequently being increasingly focused upon a consideration of activities and relationships within the workplace. Alcohol education was seen as too complicated a subject to address in the time available and alcohol was only likely to be raised when it was clearly undermining the work performance and time keeping of a trainee.

The comments above have tried to summarise the wide differences between professional groups in our four localities about alcohol and health education. Such workers respond to alcohol education possibilities in relation to their organisational role and professional training. The early Key Tutor courses have been used primarily by professional groups who focus on a limited section of the population because of their statutory responsibilities to minimise certain types of social problem. This suggests that there needs to be a major concentration of effort and resources upon training, and future courses should target generalists (primary health care workers, youth workers and teachers) more than specialists.

Like many other programmes and organisations, the South West alcohol education programme is faced with a considerable gap between a general statement of philosophy and a growing list of activities. Are these activities always consistent with the philosophy? Is the primary emphasis upon alcohol education for the general public or for those whose drinking is associated with the kind of social problems that require the intervention of statutory agencies? One mechanism for reducing this dilemma is to establish clear concrete objectives by which the priority and form of future activities can be judged.

An optimistic conclusion?

Dorn and South, in their review of articles, reports, books and previous reviews on the mass media and alcohol, provide what they call "a pessimistic conclusion" because:

> "The alcohol field (it appears to us) provides an arena within which two apparently opposing, actually complementary conceptions of 'responsible' lifestyles are currently being articulated. One such conception emphasises temperance (in both its general and alcohol-specific meanings) and social discipline, whereas the other, in more liberal fashion, emphasises the individual's right to choose (including the right to purchase alcohol, and even to drink to excess, as long as one bears the consequences).... While the advocates of these two conceptions of the good life disagree with each other, their disagreement has a strangely static quality about it - a quality found amongst those who have 'agreed to differ'. One consequence of the hegemony of this dialogue on responsibility ('choice' vs 'discipline') is the exclusion of conceptions of the health

education audience that do not fit into that dialogue."[29]

The SAUS research team feels this is too harsh a judgement to apply to those already involved in alcohol education in the South West. Most individuals cannot be neatly allocated to one end or the other of the 'choice' vs 'discipline' spectrum. In particular, all Councils on Alcoholism in the South West are engaged in various forms of education and none of them pursue a strict abstinence approach towards all their clients. The old certainties and the disease model are being abandoned and new innovative approaches are being tested.

However, education still means very different things to different people. The resultant debate is having to occur in the context of uncertainty about the balance of roles and responsibilities between the voluntary and statutory sectors. The end result is that the world of alcohol counselling and alcohol education can appear to outsiders as rather narrow and overly interested in its internal disagreements. Dorn and South went on to argue that:

> "it would make better sense for alcohol educators to stop talking amongst themselves and to start listening to their audiences."[30]

The main audience for the South West alcohol education programme is the varied and diverse residents of the South West. However, this enormous audience will often be contacted through the mediation of a wide range of professionals who work in the region. This smaller audience of professionals is also varied and also needs to be listened to and not just lectured at. Our optimism comes from a belief that this is increasingly being recognised by those most involved in the programme, irrespective of where they would locate themselves on the 'choice' vs 'discipline' spectrum.

References

1. See for example Seabrook, J. (1984), The idea of neighbourhood, Pluto Press, London.

2. This issue is discussed in detail by Dorn, N. (1983), Alcohol,

188

youth and the state, Croom Helm, London; and Dorn, N. and South, N. (1983), Message in a bottle, Gower, Aldershot.

3. Dorn (op cit), pp 210-211.

4. Balding, J. (1984), "The use of a general questionnaire on health related behaviour in curriculum planning in secondary schools", pp 115-122 from Health education and youth: a review of research and developments edited by George Campbell, Falmer Press, Lewes.

5. Franklin, A. (1985), Pub drinking and the licensed trade: a study of drinking cultures and local community in two areas of South West England, School for Advanced Urban Studies, University of Bristol, Occasional Paper No 21.

6. Mass-Observation (1943), The pub and the people: a Worktown study, Victor Gollancz, London.

7. Ibid, pp 20-21.

8. Ibid, p 167.

9. Wilson, P. (1980), Drinking in England and Wales, Office of Population Censuses and Surveys, HMSO, London.

10. Saunders, W. (1984), 'Alcohol use in Britain: how much is too much?', Health Education Journal, Vol 43, Nos 2 and 3, pp 67-70.

11. Sabey, B. and Staughton, G. (1980), The drinking road user in Great Britain, Transport and Road Research Laboratory, Supplementary Report 616.

12. Plant, M. (1985), Women, drinking and pregnancy, Tavistock, London.

13. Plant, M. (1985), 'Drinking and pregnancy', Alcohol Concern, Vol 1, No 3, pp 9-10.

14. Alcohol Concern, Vol 1, No 5, 1 pp 9-10.

15. Seely, S. (1985), 'It's hard to put a label on a disease and make it stick', Guardian, 19 April, p 16. See also Seely, S., Freed,

Silverstone and Rippere (forthcoming) <u>Diet-related diseases: the modern epidemic</u>, Croom Helm, London.

16. Gill, O. (1977), <u>Luke Street: housing policy, conflict and the creation of the delinquent area</u>, Macmillan, London, p 184.

17. Lawson, A. (1980), 'Taking the decision to remove the child from the family', <u>The Journal of Social Welfare Law</u>, May, pp 141-163.

18. Hope, T. (1985), <u>Implementing crime prevention measures</u>, Home Office Research Study 86, HMSO, London.

19. The police in Plymouth have used similar techniques to provide an indication of the spread of drink related public disorder in the city centre.

20. Hope (op cit), p 57.

21. Coleman, A. (1985), <u>Utopia on trial: vision and reality in planned housing</u>, Shipman, London.

22. The seminar was run by the Institute for the Study of Drug Dependence.

23. The importance of this issue is fully discussed in Lipsky, M. (1980), <u>Street level bureaucracy</u>, Russell Sage, New York.

24. Shaw, S., Cartwright, A., Spratley, T. and Harwin, J. (1978), <u>Responding to drinking problems</u>, Croom Helm, London.

25. Schools Council/HEC (1977), <u>All about me, for ages 5-8</u> and <u>Think well, for ages 9-13</u>, Nelson, Walton-on-Thames.

26. Some of the reasons for the growth of interest in social education are discussed in Varlaam, C. ed (1984), <u>Rethinking transition: educational innovation and the transition to adult life</u>, The Falmer Press, Lewes.

27. Thompson Report (1982), <u>Experience and participation: report of the review group on the youth service in England</u>, HMSO, London, Cmnd 8686, p 68.

28. Manpower Services Commission (1982), <u>Youth Task Group Report</u>, MSC, Sheffield.

29. Dorn and South (op cit), p 37.

30. Ibid, p 38.